Five Levers
to Improve
Learning

Thank you for working with our office. We hope this book finds you at the right place at the right time. Our wish is that you share this book with others once you are finished with it.

OFFICE of
INNOVATION
for **EDUCATION**

479-575-4499
OIE@uark.edu
InnovativeEd.org
@InnoEdOIE

Five Levers to Improve Learning

How to Prioritize for Powerful Results in Your School

TONY FRONTIER &
JAMES RICKABAUGH

Alexandria, Virginia USA

1703 N. Beauregard St. • Alexandria, VA 22311-1714 USA
Phone: 800-933-2723 or 703-578-9600 • Fax: 703-575-5400
Website: www.ascd.org • E-mail: member@ascd.org
Author guidelines: www.ascd.org/write

Gene R. Carter, *Executive Director;* Richard Papale, *Publisher;* Laura Lawson, *Acquisitions Editor;* Julie Houtz, *Director, Book Editing & Production;* Deborah Siegel, *Editor;* Lindsey Smith, *Graphic Designer;* Mike Kalyan, *Production Manager;* Valerie Younkin, *Production Designer;* Kyle Steichen, *Production Specialist*

Printed in the United States of America. Cover art © 2014 ASCD. ASCD publications present a variety of viewpoints. The views expressed or implied in this book should not be interpreted as official positions of the Association. All referenced trademarks are the property of their respective owners.

All web links in this book are correct as of the publication date below but may have become inactive or otherwise modified since that time. If you notice a deactivated or changed link, please e-mail books@ascd.org with the words "Link Update" in the subject line. In your message, please specify the web link, the book title, and the page number on which the link appears.

ASCD Member Book No. FY14-4B (Jan. 2014, PSI+) ASCD Member Books mail to Premium (P), Select (S), and Institutional Plus (I+) members on this schedule: Jan, PSI+; Feb, P; Apr, PSI+; May P; Jul, PSI+; Aug, P; Sep, PSI+; Nov, PSI+; Dec, P. For up-to-date details on membership, see www.ascd.org/membership.

PAPERBACK ISBN: 978-1-4166-1754-9   ASCD product # 114002

Also available as an e-book (see Books in Print for the ISBNs).

Quantity discounts: 10–49 copies, 10%; 50+ copies, 15%; for 1,000 or more copies, call 800-933-2723, ext. 5634, or 703-575-5634. For desk copies: www.ascd.org/deskcopy

Library of Congress Cataloging-in-Publication Data
Frontier, Tony.
    Five levers to improve learning : how to prioritize for powerful results in your school / Tony Frontier and James Rickabaugh.
        pages cm
    Includes bibliographical references and index.
    ISBN 978-1-4166-1754-9 (pbk. : alk. paper) 1. School improvement programs.
2. Academic achievement. I. Rickabaugh, James. II. Title.
    LB2822.8.F756 2014
    371.2'07–dc23
                                                                        2013038024

23 22 21 20 19 18 17 16 15 14 13   1 2 3 4 5 6 7 8 9 10 11 12

Lever—n., from Old French, *to raise*; from Latin, *to make light.*
1. a simple machine used to transmit force. 2. a handle used to adjust or operate a mechanism. 3. a means or device used to accomplish something.

"Give me a lever long enough and a fulcrum on which to place it, and I shall move the world."
—*Archimedes, ancient Greek scientist and inventor*

"There is no world. There's only 6 billion understandings of it. And if you change one person's understanding of what they're capable of, you've changed the whole thing."
—*Drew Dudley, 21st century author, speaker, and leadership development expert*

Five Levers to Improve Learning
How to Prioritize for Powerful Results in Your School

Introduction: Schools, Leadership, and Change

Vignette 1: A New School

Based on the premise that "smaller is better," Willow Wood School District was awarded a significant grant to create a small high school, with funding provided for various structural changes that would be required. The grant application had described how the smaller environment would create a more connected, personalized learning experience for students.

In the initial months the district addressed complex logistical details and brought in architects to plan for changes to a wing of an existing high school. The district's IT team began to plan for a new computer network. A planning committee was formed to discuss the mission and vision of the new school. It was decided that teachers would be trained in a comprehensive instructional methodology emphasizing authentic problem solving and workplace readiness. The district brought in a consultant to assist with marketing to appeal to students with an interest in 21st century manufacturing and international business. A school principal was selected. A name, Global Prosperity Academy, was chosen because it aligned with the adopted mission of providing an international education that would prepare students to thrive in a global economy.

Six months before the opening of the new school, staff members were hired from the existing high school, and they were empowered to make a number of decisions related to curriculum and school structure. The intent was to develop a curriculum whereby students could focus on one of three sets of courses emphasizing workplace-readiness skills, global awareness, or engineering. Each student would have a laptop. The staff chose to implement a block schedule, and rather than using a traditional report card, they decided to use a new standards-based report card. An online curriculum development tool was selected for teachers to develop and track their curricula.

By the start of the school year, the building was ready, and students were enrolled. Staff had attended two summer workshops to gain a better understanding of authentic problem-solving strategies and workplace-readiness skills. At a parent meeting a few days before school began, the new standards-based report card was distributed, along with a pamphlet explaining the philosophy of the school and its mission statement. The facility looked great, and the community was energized by the concept of a new, small school with a global focus and lots of computers.

On opening day, a crew from a local television station pulled in front of the school, and a reporter spoke with students and others about the opportunities offered by the Global Prosperity Academy. The story that aired that night featured a close-up of the school's gleaming new sign; a few interviews with excited parents, the principal, and hopeful students; a shot of the impressive computer lab; and a closing scene showing a group of students heading inside as the first bell rang. The prospects of the Global Prosperity Academy had stirred tremendous excitement.

Unfortunately, that excitement quickly waned. After a few months it was clear that student achievement was no better than it had been at the large high school—and attendance rates were actually worse. The curriculum was never fully developed around the identified mission and purpose, and factions formed between what students perceived to be the high-achieving engineering group and the low-achieving workplace-readiness group. Two years later, the school was moved to a new site and completely reorganized. The enthusiasm of the early days gave way to finger-pointing, blame, and frustration.

Vignette 2: A New Kitchen

If you've ever undertaken a kitchen remodeling project, you understand the complexity of the process. It typically begins with an expressed need or concern: not enough room for the family, too few cabinets, outdated décor; or perhaps it's just time for a change. For the next several months, a conversation unfolds about what to do. You look at catalogs and web pages and bring in contractors to share their perspectives. As you gather quotes, sticker shock starts the process all over again. You discuss the long-term impact of the decision on finances and do some form of cost-benefit analysis on the back of an envelope or, perhaps, in a meticulously designed Excel spreadsheet. You consult the bank and hire a contractor, and finally the work begins.

For the next several months, your life is total chaos. Fast-food containers pile up in the trash, and dishes in the bathroom sink become the new normal. The contractor realizes that a product is on back order, and the electrician, who was supposed to come a few weeks ago, is out on another emergency call.

Just as you are about to give up hope, progress is made, and you see the new kitchen actually starting to take shape. Walls are painted; the sink works. You move your dishes into the new cabinets, turn on the new stove, and are excited at the prospect of actually using your new kitchen. You write the final check for the contractor and revel in the fact that the remodeling job is complete.

You are thrilled with the result. There's more room, it's more comfortable, and the space looks great.

That evening, you prepare your first meal in the remodeled space. You grab your grandmother's pot roast recipe from a folder on the new shelf. You've made the recipe dozens of times and are anxious to prepare it in the new kitchen. You pull several shiny new pans out of the impressive cabinets, fill a measuring cup with water from the new sink, take vegetables and a roast out of your new stainless steel refrigerator, steam the vegetables on the new stove, and place the roast in your new oven. The table is set. The digital timer announces that the roast is finished, so you take it out of the oven and set it on a hot pad on the impressive granite countertop. You are ready to eat. You sit down at the table and serve yourself. You take the first bite of the roast, close your eyes, and begin to chew.

You open your eyes. A feeling of disappointment washes over you as you realize that the food tastes exactly the same as it did when you prepared it in the old kitchen. It's good, but not great. It's your grandmother's recipe, but it's still not your grandmother's pot roast. Your 7-year-old complains that he doesn't like it. The 10-year-old asks why you didn't make it like Grandma does. Although the kitchen looks very different than it did before, the time, the effort, and the resources invested in the remodeling process didn't translate into better results.

"This tastes the way it did in the old kitchen," you sigh.

"Why would remodeling the kitchen make the food taste better?" asks your 10-year-old.

When we read these anecdotes, we're disappointed that the shift to a smaller school didn't have the intended results. The district invested time, effort, and resources in improving a school, and the initiative was unsuccessful. However, when we read about the kitchen remodel, we're surprised that anyone would expect the food to taste any better. Why is it that when a school is restructured we expect an increase in student learning, yet when we remodel a kitchen we understand that the quality of the food won't necessarily improve?

This book provides a framework for thinking about school improvement in a way that aligns effort and results for a successful outcome. But before we outline the basic components of the framework, let's consider the broader context surrounding current reform efforts.

Standing at the Crossroads

Barely two generations ago, the United States led the world in educational attainment. By the end of the civil rights movement, children had access to near-universal public education through high school. Meanwhile, most other developed countries were positioned to educate only a portion of their children and youth. American achievement was the envy of the world.

Two generations ago, the design of public education in the United States was generally well aligned with the economic needs of the nation. A minority of students were educated at high levels, and a majority were well prepared to enter an adult work environment that was highly structured, that suited workers who could tolerate repetitive tasks and needed close supervision and direction, and that accommodated those who were not prepared to solve complex problems. People who were educated at higher levels generally were responsible for supervising and managing the rest.

Two generations ago students could leave formal education knowing most of what they would need to succeed as adults. Even students who left the school system before high school graduation could find work that paid well enough to raise a family and enjoy a middle-class life. As Harvard professor Roland Barth has stated,

> Fifty years ago high school graduates left school knowing 75% of what they would ever need to know in order to function successfully in the workplace, in their families and communities. Today, the estimate is that our high school graduates leave knowing only 2% of what they need to know, leaving 98% yet to come. It is not that high school graduates know less than their counterparts back in the 1950's; in fact, they know far more. But today, a basic kit of knowledge just does not cut it anymore. (1997, p. 56)

Two generations ago, most Americans viewed education as a key investment in building a better future for the nation and its communities. Taxpayers were generally willing to invest in infrastructure and operational costs to ensure that schools were able to accomplish the mission they had been given. Schools as institutions, although criticized, were generally seen as providing a path to a better future than the life enjoyed by the previous generation.

The world has changed—dramatically. Most experts agree that the U.S. education system has not improved significantly over the past decade or more (Ravitch, 2010). Test scores are generally flat, and many view the federal and state policies designed to move the system forward as having fallen far short and maybe even being a distraction from a focus that might have produced better results.

Meanwhile, other developed countries have invested strategically in their educational systems, are seeing significant progress, and are growing their capacity to do even better. The U.S. system that not long ago was the envy of the world has slipped on international rankings in academic subject areas to at or below the international average (Organisation for Economic Cooperation and Development [OECD], 2010). Other countries now are educating an ever larger portion of their youth, whereas the stubbornly high dropout rate in the United States increasingly leaves us educating a comparatively smaller cohort of its youth (Tucker, 2011). Even the performance of our best students no longer stacks up well against the best in other countries. For example, the portion of students in the United States performing at the highest levels on international exams is smaller than in some developing countries, including Mexico (OECD, 2010). It is not so much that U.S. education has fallen back as it is that other countries are improving at a faster rate and achieving better results with their work. The current U.S. system is inefficient in that we are spending hundreds of millions of dollars to remediate students who fail to learn.

Each year special education classes are filled with tens of thousands of students who perhaps would not have to be there if they had been taught, from the start of their schooling, in the ways that they learn best. Ironically, when students finally find themselves identified and placed in such classes, the focus becomes doing that very thing—teaching them in the ways they learn best.

As noted, our national dropout rate has remained stubbornly high. Yet students who decide to leave high school before graduation overwhelmingly report that their reasons for leaving were not that the work was too hard but, rather, that they found the work to be boring and not relevant or useful to the lives they envision. Meanwhile, of students who graduate from high school and choose to enroll in two-year colleges, 75 percent must enroll in remedial courses in math or English or both (National Center for Public Policy and Higher Education, 2010).

The well-paying but relatively low-skill jobs of the past—for which a large portion of students were prepared and which once supported the middle class—are gone. The jobs have been either absorbed by technology or shipped to places where labor is less expensive and less organized. No longer can a student leave formal education at the end of high school (or before) and expect to gain and hold a job that will support a middle-class lifestyle.

The public's willingness to pay for today's educational system also is waning. The cost of education in the United States is among the highest in the developed world. Yet the results are at best average, and, as noted, they appear to be slipping as other countries invest in and improve their systems. Taxpayers increasingly ask whether they are getting a reasonable return on their investment. Line items for education in the federal and state budgets are seen as expenditures to be minimized and contained rather than as an investment that will yield a high return. As the U.S. population ages and fewer taxpayers have children in schools, this challenge will grow. We must find ways to increase the efficiency and productivity of our schools if we hope to maintain community support in terms of both goodwill and funding.

Meanwhile, educators are being held to higher levels of accountability than ever before. No Child Left Behind legislation created new levels of accountability for schools to address the needs of all students. Race to the Top grants move that accountability to each individual teacher, and new policies related to teacher evaluation place teachers under higher levels of scrutiny. At the same time, contrary to cynics' perceptions, teachers and administrators work extremely hard—both in and out of their schools—to address student needs.

In the middle of this expanding challenge, reformers at the federal, state, and even local levels too often become preoccupied with supposed "silver bullet" solutions that address aspects of the system yet hold little leverage and even less promise of making a real difference in student learning. These solutions often sound plausible and make intuitive sense. Unfortunately, such solutions frequently focus on the wrong levers and result in little if any improvement. Yet they can cost hundreds of millions of dollars, waste valuable time, defeat teachers, and demotivate students before losing favor and being abandoned.

Despite these seismic shifts, the U.S. educational system continues much as it did when students' prospects after high school were much better and more predictable. As a result, we risk having the current system underprepare large segments of the student population, creating a permanent underclass without the skills necessary to succeed in today's workplace while hundreds of thousands of excellent-paying jobs that require higher skills go unfilled, even in recessionary times (McKinsey & Company, 2009). Today's schools and districts must consider different ways to leverage their capacity to educate all students at high levels.

A Predictable Pattern

Look at the characteristics of School A and School B in the following table. Both schools are a part of the same district and are only a few miles apart. At which school would you predict higher levels of student achievement?

School A	School B
Charter school	Public school
1-to-1 laptops	1 computer lab
Standards-based report card	Traditional report card
Some gender-separate classrooms	Co-ed classrooms
Block schedule	52-minute periods
Extended school day	Standard school day
Online norm-referenced formative assessments 3 × year	Norm-referenced formative assessments
Collaborative release time	No collaborative release time
19 students per class	24 students per class
185 total students	628 total students

The hundreds of educators with whom we've shared this table in workshops and classes tend to be fairly evenly divided when looking at these two schools: about one-third argue for School A, one-third argue for School B, and one-third argue that the information is insufficient to enable a prediction about achievement. In support of each argument they often cite anecdotal evidence of an initiative that succeeded or failed, identify their support or disdain for components recently adopted or approved by their school boards, and sometimes even cite specific pieces of research to support their position.

Then, they are told that there is more to the story of these two schools. In addition to the structural characteristics listed in the first table, there are a number of other differences between School A and School B. These differences are listed in the following table.

School A	School B
Ambiguous mission and purpose	Clearly defined mission and purpose and utilization of measures aligned to both
No published, articulated curriculum	Prioritized curriculum and learning goals
Exclusive utilization of judgmental feedback from teachers to students	Developmental feedback and expectation of mastery over time on targeted goals
Didactic, nondifferentiated instructional methods	Flexible, student-responsive instructional methods
Lecture utilized almost exclusively	Instructional strategies aligned to learner's needs
Low time-on-task for student learning	High time-on-task for student learning
Does not use data to inform improvement efforts	Data systematically used by students, teachers, and administrators to inform improvement efforts
Collaborative time utilized to discuss logistics and scheduling	Frequent dialogue among teachers linking achievement and perception data to action planning for curriculum, instruction, and assessment
Teacher supervision and evaluation utilized in a punitive manner, and only after parent complaints	Feedback actively sought among teachers and administrators in continuous efforts to improve their practice
Low academic press among staff; low expectations among students; general mistrust among administration, teachers, and students.	High academic press among staff; high levels of support and trust; high expectations for learning among administration, teachers, and students

At this point, nearly all educators say that School B would demonstrate dramatically better learning outcomes than School A. Rather than arguing for why they think School B would demonstrate higher levels of achievement, they simply talk about how nice it would be to work there. They don't feel the need to argue in favor of School B because, given these additional descriptors, it is the obvious choice.

Why is it that when we implement structural changes, such as those listed in the first set of descriptors, we expect students to learn more? Too often, the effort put forth, the political chips spent, and the resources allocated to make these structural changes result in few, if any, meaningful differences in educational practices or student learning. These structural changes are one type of leverage that can be used to influence student learning, and the appeal of this lever is strong. It is concrete in that the current structure and the desired structure can be clearly articulated and explained to community members, parents, and boards of education. Changes such as moving to a block schedule, adding more computers, or developing a new report card fit neatly into strategic plans, and their implementation processes have clearly defined starting and ending dates. However, we argue that these types of changes often produce the least amount of leverage in terms of improving student learning.

Maximizing Effectiveness by Engaging in the *Right* Work

This book isn't about engaging in *more work*; it is about a simple but powerful framework to ensure that we are engaged in the *right work* to prioritize efforts to develop classrooms, schools, and districts that make the fullest possible use of our collective capacity to improve student learning. This book is about identifying—and letting go of—initiatives that will likely languish or fail, and identifying and embracing those that are likely to lead to student success. It is about becoming aware of efforts that will result in what we call *leverage advantages* as compared to those that can result in *leverage errors*.

Leverage Advantages

A lever is a means or device used to accomplish something that otherwise might not have been possible. In physical terms, a lever is useful because it dramatically increases the amount of weight that can be lifted on one end of the lever given a limited amount of force applied to the other end. Through the intentional use of a fulcrum and a plane, a lever redistributes force in a manner that makes the impossible, possible. Archimedes carries this concept to the absurd (but technically plausible) extreme with his assertion that if you give him a lever long enough and a fulcrum on which to place it, he will move the world.

In organizational terms, we describe levers as the key areas where we exert influence in order to obtain a desired goal. A banker may talk about how she can leverage assets and debt to improve profits. A football coach may talk about how he can leverage specific strengths in his offense to score more touchdowns. A teacher may talk about how she can leverage formative assessment strategies to improve each student's learning.

When intent, effort, and results are aligned across a school's planning processes, the school accelerates toward a desired outcome with a level of efficiency and effectiveness that otherwise would not have been possible. We call this alignment the *leverage advantage*. For example, ensuring kids arrive at school safely and on time is important. To make this happen efficiently, schools use buses, schedule routes, and assign designated stops to ensure a dependable path toward the intended outcome. The alignment between intent and effort creates a leverage advantage to obtain the desired result of safety and punctuality.

Leverage Errors

In contrast to a leverage advantage, a *leverage error* occurs when intent, effort, and results are misaligned. Suppose an initiative were put on the table to improve student achievement by painting the buses a brighter color and having them drop students off on the other side of the building. Although the intent of the initiative—improving student achievement—is important, the effort required to engage in the recommended action would likely fail to affect student learning. This example illustrates an obvious disconnect among intent, effort, and results. If the intent is to improve student achievement, there are more efficient and effective ways to reach the intended outcome. But we *do* spend a lot of time in the field painting buses (metaphorically speaking) and expecting improved student learning. In his book *Visible Learning*, John Hattie (2009) reports the results of the largest synthesis of research ever conducted in the field of education. In his explanation of some of his most surprising—and most important—findings, he writes the following:

> One of the most fascinating discoveries throughout my research
> for this book is discovering that many of the most debated issues
> are the ones with the least effects. It is a powerful question to ask
> why such issues as class size, tracking, retention, school choice,

summer schools, and school uniforms command such heated discussion and strong claims. Such cosmetic or "coat of paint" reforms are too common. (p. 33)

In other words, we are more prone to the leveraging error than we think. We argue that this occurs, in part, not because educators lack a shared model for talking about the *magnitude* of change we seek, but because we lack a shared model for talking about the components—or levers—within class-rooms, schools, and districts that inform *where* we should focus our efforts to accomplish the change we seek.

Navigating Change

Whether you are leading change in your classroom, department, school, district, or state, change is always complex and rarely easy. A variety of researchers and authors (see, for example, Burns, 1978; Davidovich, Nikolay, Laugerman, & Commodore, 2010; Fullan, 2001; Hall & Hord, 2010; Heifetz & Linsky, 2002; Marzano, Waters, & McNulty, 2005) have made significant con-tributions to our collective understanding of the characteristics of different types of change and how change does—or does not—occur. Research and theory on change provide insight into two critically important areas: (1) the magnitude of the change and (2) the leadership practices associated with change. These two areas inform the outcomes leaders expect as a result of their planning and the leadership behaviors most likely to help the organi-zation attain those outcomes. Unfortunately they do not provide guidance on how to determine which initiatives will most likely result in improved student learning so that the initiatives can be prioritized accordingly.

Magnitude of change describes the extent to which the change requires individuals to use different knowledge or skills or adopt new disposi-tions and ways of thinking in order to successfully move the organization forward. *Leadership practices associated with change* include the specific things that leaders do to help organizations balance the need for appropri-ate levels of challenge, so they can move beyond their current state, while supporting the development of the new knowledge and skills required for success. In addition, effective leaders are responsive to the people who are a part of the change. People tend to respond to change in fairly predict-able ways. The more that leaders understand the needs people have when embarking on a change process, how those needs differ depending on each individual's perception of the magnitude of the change, and the extent to which those individuals believe the change will help them be more successful, the better leaders can ensure each person's success.

Researchers have developed various ways to think about magnitude of change, and their work can help leaders consider the extent to which they need to challenge and support the organization's capacity to move to the next level of practice, recognize the specific leadership behaviors that are more and less associated with achieving success across the magnitude of change, and consider the most effective strategy necessary to implement change. For example, Marzano et al. (2005) have made an invaluable contribution to the field by identifying specific leadership behaviors associated with what they call "first-order change" and "second-order change." Here is how Marzano and his colleagues characterize these magnitudes of change:

First-Order Change...	Second-Order Change...
• Is an extension of the past. • Fits with existing paradigms. • Includes existing knowledge and skills. • Is consistent with values and norms. • May be seen by others as obvious and necessary.	• Is a break from the past. • Lies outside existing paradigms. • Requires new knowledge and skills. • Conflicts with existing values and norms. • May be resisted by others as irrelevant.

Heifetz and Linsky (2002) succinctly describe the risks and opportunities involved in successfully leading "adaptive change" as opposed to "technical change." Here is how they characterize these representations of magnitude of change:

Technical Change...	Adaptive Change...
• Requires changes in routine behaviors and preferences. • Uses existing knowledge and skills. • Is directed from above. • Deploys existing competence in a different context.	• Requires new ways of thinking about the organization's work. • Requires changes in knowledge, skills, and dispositions. • Is internalized and implemented by stakeholders. • Recognizes that existing competence may no longer be relevant or adequate.

In this book we use the terms *transactional change* and *transformational change* as initially coined by James Burns (1978) because we believe they encompass many of the key concepts associated with both *first-order* and *technical change* as well as with *second-order* and *adaptive change*. We've also added a third component to help frame the ideas in this book: *status quo management.*

Planning for Status Quo, Transactional, and Transformational Outcomes

Schools are required to plan for hundreds of outcomes—for example, at the district and community level, to determine the tax levy or to establish a vision to guide the next 10 years of effort; at the building level, to ensure elementary students understand how to line up on the recently reconfigured playground or to establish building goals; or by a collaborative teaching team, to plan an annual field trip to the state capital or to develop a new instructional unit.

Regardless of the group engaged in the planning or the lever that they are attempting to use, we contend that planning involves one of three intended outcomes: maintenance of the status quo, transactional change, or transformational change. Figure I.1 lists the characteristics of these three outcomes, examples, and the types of questions often asked when working toward them. The extent of leaders' understanding of, and ability to articulate, the outcomes they are *planning toward* will influence the effort they put forth and the results they achieve.

Planning for maintaining the status quo occurs when people (1) consider the outcomes that result from current organizational efforts to be acceptable and (2) believe the associated processes are effective and efficient. Planning for the status quo largely entails practices associated with effective management, including clarity of tasks, delineation of responsibilities, and streamlined work flow. Developing a schedule for busing students in a new school year is an example of planning for the status quo. People are satisfied with the current processes and outcomes; the local bus service fulfills its role as designed, in that the buses pick up the children and deliver them to school each day. Each year a considerable amount of logistical planning needs to occur to maintain the status quo, including enrolling students, identifying children in need of services, communicating with the bus

Figure I.1 | Three Outcomes of Planning

Outcomes	Examples	Associated Planning Questions
Status Quo Management • Maintain existing expectations for performance • Maintain existing roles, structures • Maintain existing purpose, products, tasks • Emphasis on updating annual products and tasks	• "Rolling over" processes and procedures from the previous year • Keeping track of and tabulating grades in the same manner as in the past • Completing teacher evaluation processes and forms in the same manner as in the past	• What rules, processes, and procedures need to be followed? • What dates and deadlines must be met? • What information needs to be communicated so this runs smoothly again?
Transactional Change* • Exchange of skills or services valued by one group for rewards valued by another group • Group focus • Contingent rewards • Monitoring and corrective action	• Implementing a schedule change • Implementing a new way of tabulating and reporting grades • Implementing ratings from a new framework for teacher evaluation	• What new rules, processes, and procedures need to be followed? • What new dates and deadlines must be met? • What rewards and punishments will affirm or extinguish behavior?
Transformational Change* • Interaction among leaders and followers to increase capacity to meet the needs of others • Focused on the individual, to the benefit of the group • Attention to motivation • Intellectual stimulation • Supportive of autonomy	• Using class time differently to focus on rigor and student engagement • Teaching students strategies to set attainable goals based on formative assessments • Developing and using a shared language of effective instruction for teachers to use during self-reflection based on a video of their teaching	• How do we determine if students are engaged or merely compliant? • What do students believe to be true about the relationship between their effort and results? • What is the balance between formative and summative practices that supports teacher growth yet ensures accountability?

*The characteristics of transactional change and transformational change are based on J. M. Burns (1978) and B. M. Bass (1985).

company, matching children with the most efficient routes, telling parents when their child will be picked up, and so on. If all students are picked up, all the buses arrive on time, and the services work as well as they did the previous year, success means the status quo has been maintained.

Planning for transactional change requires addressing a different set of variables. Those involved in planning can draw on existing competence to facilitate the change, but a different set of transactions will need to occur to yield the same result. For example, due to lower enrollment and fewer students requiring bus services, nine bus routes may need to be consolidated down to six. This shift will likely involve significant planning and communication. It may require a change in terms of service with the busing company and will require different routes and pickup points and times than in the past. The skills used to create routes and communicate pickup information will continue to work, but the schedule will look different. Buses may pick up children significantly earlier or later than before. Although the adults had to engage in a different planning process and students had to adjust to a new schedule, the students' experience and outcomes remain largely the same. Success involves a different set of transactions that yield results that are similar to what was obtained in the past.

Planning for transformational change requires those implementing the change and those participating in the change to think differently about the nature of the work that they are doing. In addition, the previous skills and habits of mind are no longer useful or relevant. Extending the busing example, consider the transformational implications of planning the implementation of an online school. The concept of what it means to "bring a student to school" will require a completely new set of practices and a wide range of new beliefs by the adults involved in planning. Planning bus routes and communicating pickup times are suddenly irrelevant and are replaced by new conversations—and different types of strategic thinking—about what it means for a student to be *at* school. Students will need to reconceptualize what it means to be *ready for school*, *in class*, and *at school*. Adults and children will need to navigate an experience that used to be governed by seat time and is now governed by outcomes. The premise of the system has been transformed, but the most important transformations will occur in the perceptions regarding how the teachers see themselves as teachers and the students see themselves as learners.

"The Single Most Common Source of Leadership Failure"

In their book *Leadership on the Line*, Ronald Heifetz and Marty Linsky (2002) argue that "the single most common source of leadership failure is that people treat adaptive challenges like technical problems" (p. 14). We agree, and for the purposes of this book we shift the semantics to state that leadership failure is associated with treating *transformational* challenges with *transactional* solutions. In these scenarios, people confronting a problem look to leadership for a quick, simple fix—a new form to fill out, a different schedule, a new report card, a new textbook. Dozens of examples illustrate how enticing—and seemingly intuitive—transactional solutions can be: *If we just had a different form, then we'd be able to change people's perceptions of the program. If the 3rd graders ate lunch earlier, then math scores would improve. If we had a new report card, then concerns about grading would go away. If we could put all the kids with characteristic X in the same classroom, then achievement would improve.* In each of these scenarios, an external portion of the equation is adjusted so that people can maintain the status quo or engage in a different set of transactions with the hope that others will change their behavior and obtain better results.

Education is littered with well-intended transactional solutions to problems that, in reality, require transformational changes in practice. Too often, the surface-level changes that were implemented resulted in neither improved organizational capacity nor improved student learning. Here, the leveraging error is the result of a misconception of the magnitude of the challenge; the lever was too short to generate the force required to transform practice. But what about scenarios in which significant efforts for transformation were sought and the desired results were obtained, yet students' experience remained unchanged?

Where Will the Change Occur?

Treating transformational challenges with transactional solutions is only one way that school leaders' significant efforts do not leverage organizational capacity to influence student learning. Another critical dimension to this challenge is the *where*—that is, where within the organization the leader attempts to implement change. It is not only the size of the lever that must align to the magnitude of change; the lever must also align to the area of the organization where the intended and the enacted change will provide the greatest advantage. Without a framework for thinking clearly about the magnitude of change and the area that will provide the greatest leverage to make that change possible, it is easy to miscalculate both the size of the lever and its placement. This miscalculation is not exclusive to overworked department chairs or novice principals. Everyone is subject to these leveraging errors.

Case in point: In 2000, the Bill and Melinda Gates Foundation embarked on a $2 billion quest to improve high school graduation rates. Educational historian Diane Ravitch (2010) explains the essence of the foundation's strategy as follows:

> The Gates initiative began when the small-schools movement had become the leading edge of school reform in urban districts. The movement's ardent adherents believed that small schools were the cure to the problems of urban education. They said that students got lost in large high schools, that they would respond positively to the personalized attention they received in a small high school, and that they would thus be motivated to study, stay in school, graduate, and go to college. The foundation agreed with this diagnosis. (pp. 204–205)

In essence, the foundation's logic was this: If students attended smaller high schools, then their achievement would improve and they would be more likely to graduate. By 2008, the foundation abandoned its strategy of small-school reform. Results showed some increases in attendance rates but lower test scores in mathematics and reading. As Ravitch explains, the foundation acknowledged that its "emphasis on school structure" was not sufficient to invoke the changes required to improve achievement and career readiness (p. 211). In this scenario, the foundation addressed a transformational challenge through a transactional solution. Schedules were changed, schools were broken into smaller component parts, but students' learning experiences remained largely the same.

Although the intent was to create school environments that were more caring, the initiative was conceived to address a structural problem (schools are too large), and the most pervasive efforts were directed toward the goal of creating smaller schools. Although the school structures were indeed transformed, the core components of student experience merely extended the status quo.

Going back to our earlier kitchen analogy, not only do we educators continue to remodel the kitchen, we're continuously surprised that the food does not taste any better. The paradox of education reform is this: *The levers that are good at changing schools are often least associated with improving student learning.* In other words, too often we remodel the kitchen when we would have had more impact if we had simply put some salt and pepper on the table.

The Five Levers

We've all been there. We reach the point at the data retreat or the strategic planning meeting when it is time to stop describing areas of need and start identifying solutions that will improve student learning. Ideas put on the table may include smaller class sizes, more instructional time, a different schedule, better methods of identifying students for specific programs, or a new report card. All of these options carry the potential for significant change. They seem like logical steps toward improvement. Unfortunately, each of these suggestions likely will fail to produce significant improvements in achievement. As good as they sound, they miss—or fail to prioritize—the characteristics of initiatives that result in improved learning.

In working with students, educators, school boards, and policymakers, and in conducting and using research throughout our careers, we've found that ideas and efforts to better leverage our capacity to address student needs can be placed into five categories. These categories, or levers, reveal an often hidden framework for thinking about how educators at the individual, team, classroom, and district levels can leverage capacity and scarce resources to respond to student needs. The five levers are *structure, sample, standards, strategy,* and *self. Structure* refers to logistical components such as schedules, bells, and class size. *Sample* involves grouping of students in classrooms, programs, or learning opportunities at any given time. *Standards* include practices associated with expectations for student learning. *Strategy* refers to instructional strategies used to manage classrooms and engage students in meaningful learning experiences. *Self* includes the set of beliefs that teachers and students have about their capacity to be effective.

Each lever holds varying degrees of potential for improving student learning. Awareness of these levers can position leaders to see underlying patterns in the innovations they are considering and chart a path for more mindful, strategic, and effective organizational change. Ignoring this framework can lead to disappointment, frustration, and waste. Figure I.2 defines the five levers, lists some examples, and considers the types of planning questions associated with each of them.

In this book we argue that educators too often seek to improve student learning by engaging in misguided efforts to leverage change in schools; they adjust the structure, manipulate the sample, and even articulate new standards. Initiatives associated with these efforts will fail to yield results unless they (1) are aligned with and directly influence the connection between *standards* and instructional *strategies* used in classrooms and (2) address and build students' and teachers' conceptions of *self* as related to their capacity to achieve.

Prioritizing Efforts and Resources for Change

In our efforts to improve student achievement, where should we invest our attention, time, and resources? It is not enough to understand how to navigate and lead change, to have the resources to move initiatives forward, and to work extremely hard and be extremely dedicated. Improving schools requires us to apply our energy to efforts most likely to result in improved student learning. It is not merely doing the right work; it is aligning our work to the outcomes we seek. Some levers are well suited to creating conditions for learning but do nothing to *improve* learning. Some levers are associated with consistent, significant gains for students but are prone to the limits of the status quo and the limits of transactional leadership. Knowing which levers to pull has a tremendous impact on the results we achieve and the efficiency with which we achieve them.

Where We're Headed

The purpose of this book is to present and make accessible to educators, policymakers, and other stakeholders a framework to organize and prioritize initiatives that can improve student learning. It provides a way to distinguish between the practices most likely to improve student learning as compared to efforts that require attention, time, and resources but provide

Figure I.2 | Overview of the Five Levers

Lever	Examples	Planning Questions
Structure—Logistical components of districts, schools, and classrooms, such as schedules, staffing, and administrative processes	• School size • Class size • Annual calendar • Daily schedule	• Where should we deliver teaching? • How long should it be delivered? • What logistical issues need to be addressed?
Sample—Grouping of students in any classroom or program at any given time	• Heterogeneous vs. homogeneous grouping of students • Gender-separate classes • Access to accelerated programs	• Who should have access? • Where should specialized services be delivered? • Who should be grouped with whom?
Standards—Expectations for student learning	• State academic standards • School-level criteria for student performance • Classroom and teacher expectations for quality work	• What should be taught? • How good is good enough? • How will we know what has been learned? • How will feedback inform next efforts?
Strategy—Any one of the practices teachers use to help students deepen their understanding of content and improve their ability to use important skills	• Instructional strategies for whole-class instruction • Instructional strategies for individualized instruction • Efforts to empower students as agents in curriculum, instruction, and assessment	• How will we teach? • How will we know students have learned? • How will we build on student strengths? • How will we provide appropriate challenge for learners? • How will we provide appropriate support for learners?
Self—Beliefs that teachers and students have about their capacity to be effective	• Teacher efficacy • Autonomy support • Student confidence • Learned helplessness • Stereotype threat • Growth mind-set	• What do teachers believe to be true about students? • What do students believe to be true about teachers? • What do teachers believe about their capacity to meet student learning needs? • What do students believe about their capacity to learn?

little or no leverage to improve student learning. The chapters that follow define and describe the levers we pull to improve student learning: structure, sample, standards, strategy, and conceptions of self. We provide examples of efforts typically associated with each lever, describe their respective opportunities and pitfalls, and argue for using the levers to more mindfully engage in inquiry and action that will yield improved results. Finally, we share ways to use the five levers as you consider how to prioritize initiatives to begin, initiatives to sustain, and initiatives to let go of by describing how thinking about a campfire, a penguin, a bicycle, and a kitchen can guide educational stakeholders through the complexities of change.

If you are contemplating an educational initiative, reform effort, restructuring, or new policy, we urge you to read this book first. Not only will you be able to more insightfully evaluate proposed initiatives, you will know the questions to ask and will be able to evaluate whether the work is on the right track. As you seek to improve schools and learning, you will be able to focus your efforts more clearly and be in a better position to achieve success.

Lever 1: Structure

Vignette 1: Traditional or Block Schedule?

Frustrated with levels of achievement and attuned to teachers' concerns that kids are disengaged from their learning, a principal decides to implement a block schedule. A study committee is formed to make recommendations for either an A/B block schedule or a 4×4 block schedule. The committee convenes and six months later offers a recommendation for the 4×4 option. On the night of the initial hearing at a school board meeting, a number of parents come forward to speak against the plan. They explain that a neighboring community tried a block schedule, which resulted in a major change in the schedule for two years, followed by a reversion to the traditional schedule a few years later. A teacher representative expresses concerns about the impact of the change on planning time for some teachers. Almost two years after the principal's initial efforts, the community and the board are still discussing and debating the new schedule. It has become a divisive matter (prompting frequent letters to the editor in the community newspaper and argumentative exchanges via blog posts) and the central issue of the upcoming school board election.

Vignette 2: One-to-One Computing

In an attempt to ensure that every child is adequately prepared for the 21st century, a district undertakes an initiative to provide every student with a laptop computer. With a high level of community support, the district begins a multiyear process to purchase 5,000 laptops. The following school year it distributes computers at four pilot sites. Within a month, teachers are able to provide abundant anecdotal evidence that technology gaps among students of different economic groups have been largely addressed. More students can practice computer skills and have access to a broader range of academic resources than in the past. However, two years into the initiative, student achievement scores are unchanged, as are achievement gaps on statewide accountability tests between students of different economic groups. Several board members are concerned about the initial results and ask administrators for formal documentation that the investment is improving student achievement before continuing with the next phases of purchase and implementation.

Structure: Definition, Misconception, and Opportunity

Definition: *Structure includes logistical components such as schedules, staffing, tools, and administrative processes.*

Structural changes at the building level could include a shift to a block schedule; at the district level they could include a shift to smaller high schools; at a macro level they could include implementation of a voucher or choice system, or a districtwide move to year-round schooling. Changing structure is highly visible, and often highly political, but this type of change is enticing because it is apparent for all stakeholders and often can be articulated in a linear planning process that includes specific dates for implementation.

Misconception: *Focusing on a change in structure results in an improved learning environment.*

If all you knew about a school was that it used block scheduling or had small class sizes, what could you tell about the quality of that school? What if you knew it was a charter school or a small high school? Time and again, research shows little or no difference in student learning based on structure (Bifulco & Ladd, 2006; Milesi & Gamoran, 2006), and those studies that do find a significant effect for structural interventions often attribute the gains in student learning to changes in classroom practice associated with the change in structure—*not the structure itself* (Patall, Cooper, & Allen, 2010; Penuel, 2006). Structure tells us nothing about the quality of the processes, practices, and relationships at the classroom level where learning occurs.

Opportunity: *When thinking about structure, form should follow function.*
Structure is *related to* conditions for learning but rarely has any *effect*
on student learning. Changing school structure results in increased student
learning only under four conditions: when it (1) supports the use of more
effective instructional strategies, (2) allows for more responsive use of strategies to benefit specific groups of students, (3) removes barriers in the way
of learning opportunities for students or commitments among staff to collaborate on behalf of student learning, or (4) empowers staff and students
to better realize their capacity to teach and learn.

The Lure of Structural Change

We contend that there are two reasons why structural change is so enticing. Both are rooted in powerful mental models of where leadership should
exert effort to gain leverage in creating change. The first reason is related
to beliefs about standardization, as exemplified by the persistence of an
assembly-line mentality among many educators; the second is related to
beliefs about change that pay too little attention to the complex human
dimension that is involved.

From Teachers as Artisans to Schools as Assembly Lines

In the mid-1800s, the one-room schoolhouse was the dominant structure
of education in rural areas of the United States. Given a building with a
single classroom and a teacher, small towns and rural areas could educate
a group of children across a wide range of ages. The role of the teacher was
analogous to that of an artisan; she would work with each student or small
groups of students, tending to each component of their development over
an extended period of time until the final product emerged. Students, too,
were tapped to support the learning of other students across grades and
achievement levels.

The one-room schoolhouse was replaced by a 20th century model of
schooling that called for greater efficiency through specialization. This
model is analogous to the factory assembly line in terms of the underlying
assumptions related to technical and mechanical components of efficiency.
Just as a factory could be tooled to produce a complex mechanical product
by allowing line workers to specialize in a specific portion of the production
process, a school could produce an educated student by allowing teachers

to specialize in a specific portion of the educative process. As students "rolled through" their schooling experience, specialists would add various parts or components along the way. If all went as planned, students would emerge at the end of the line as finished products.

The impact of the assembly line on how we think about schooling cannot be overstated. The intent was to remove the human factor from the manufacturing process. Standardization, efficiency, and automaticity drove innovation and practice. The very definition of an effective manufacturing process was that it could be staffed by almost anyone who had received a minimal amount of training and still produce a uniform product. If management wanted to change the product that came off the line—for example, to produce a new model of an automobile—significant structural changes needed to occur first. Changes in the structure of the line resulted in a change in the manufacturing process, which resulted in a different product. A direct cause-and-effect relationship linked each of these steps. Retooling the line meant an outside group would come in and undertake the necessary technical changes. Workers then came back in and engaged in processes and tasks similar to those they had used in the past, yet an entirely different product would roll off the line. Although some minor adjustments may have been necessary by the workers, the time, effort, and energy invested in retooling the line resulted in the new, desired product—*every time*. In other words, leveraging the *structure* of the manufacturing process resulted in an extremely efficient change in outcomes.

Assembly-Line Thinking and the Limits of Structural Change

Obviously schools are not factories, and children are not products. Yet many educators and policymakers have an assembly-line mentality when they think about processes and outcomes related to student learning. Consider the case of the Global Prosperity Academy—the small-school restructuring effort described in the introduction to this book. In an attempt to create new outcomes for students, the district pulled on the structural lever to get different results. But unlike structural changes to the assembly line that are designed to be independent of human factors, each of these changes at the school will be effective *only if teachers and students interact with one another in different ways because of the structural change*. Through the lens of the five levers, we can gain a deeper understanding of the assumptions and actions that influenced the process and the eventual out-come exemplified by the Global Prosperity Academy:

- The "assembly line" was retooled from a larger school to a smaller school, yet a *structural* shift to a smaller school will have an effect on student learning only if teachers use the shift to create *samples* and implement *strategies* that capitalize on personalized and customized opportunities for teaching and learning.
- The report card was retooled from a traditional approach to a stan-dards-based approach. The switch was merely a *structural* change in the reporting process; the effect of a standards-based report card is accel-erated or limited by the extent to which it supports a standards-based system of teaching and learning. Such a system would include powerful, research-supported practices of (1) clearly articulating *standards* in stu-dent-friendly language, (2) using assessment formatively as a *strategy* to ensure developmental feedback and goal setting to help students learn, and (3) ensuring students develop a sense of *self-agency* by helping them connect the relationship between their effort and resultant learning (Stiggins, 2004). Further, when teachers help students to see the pur-pose and usefulness of what they are asked to learn, show them how to achieve mastery, and give them a measure of autonomy in how they will learn, students are more likely to commit to learning and to respond to a grading approach that is aligned with their effort and the progress they achieve.
- Textbooks were retooled as laptops, yet a *structural* shift from textbooks to laptops has little effect on student learning unless teachers have a firm grasp of how to use *strategies* that support technology as an instructional and learning tool and believe in the efficacy of using digital tools to improve student learning (Mouza, 2008).

As in the age-old riddle about the tree falling in the forest, we must ask ourselves the following question: If we've engaged in significant change efforts but students don't have a significantly different learning experi-ence, has anything really changed? In the next sections we consider just a few examples of structural changes that have received a lot of attention in recent years—acquisition of technology, school choice, and increased seat time—and place those components into a broader context through the five-lever framework.

Technology as a Structural Lever

Over the past three decades, schools and districts have spent billions of dollars on technology. Early iterations included having students use computers for drill and practice on skills. Computers have been presented as a way to increase student engagement, and the Internet was seen as a way to liberate students from textbooks and give them access to the world's knowledge. Some even thought that computers and other technology tools would replace teachers.

Almost every school and school system has invested in building the technology skills of teachers with the hope that their growing competence would mean greater integration of technology into instruction and increases in student learning. Technologies such as interactive whiteboards have been a favorite focus of parent groups and other fund-raising organizations, and more recently, many school districts and some states have invested in laptop computers for every student, betting that if students have greater access to technology, they will learn more and teachers will more completely transform their instructional practices to take advantage of technology tools. For many people, virtual and blended instruction has been the approach of choice to deliver on the promise of technology to increase student engagement and improve learning.

Faulty Assumptions About Technology and Learning

Unfortunately, despite the billions spent on technology, there is little evidence that the investment has paid off in a more powerful manner than most other interventions (Tamim, Bernard, Barokhovski, Abrami, & Schmid, 2011). The belief in technology as a driver for education reform rests on several assumptions: technology will increase the efficiency of instruction and thus lead to more learning; technology will make instruction more effective or at least more engaging; and giving students greater access to technology will result in their having greater ownership of their learning and thus better outcomes. Each of these assumptions seems reasonable, but technology has not been proven to have the intended impact.

It is correct that technology has increased efficiency in some areas of school operation. A wide array of administrative tasks, from budget management and library media organization to student attendance, has become more efficient, but these processes are not directly connected to student learning. Technology has enabled teachers to develop and store lessons and related documents digitally, thus making retrieval and updating more efficient; but again, these changes do not, by themselves, increase student performance.

Technology's role in making instruction more effective and engaging is also questionable. Lecture remains the most common instructional delivery mode in the United States. Lessons may be supported by PowerPoint presentations and digitally stored videos, but these approaches retain and depend on the legacy instructional model. Without changes in the strategies teachers use to deliver and support instruction, too often technology simply changes the platform for instruction, *not the instruction itself*. Consequently, the results have not changed. At the extremes are teachers who use interactive whiteboards in the same way they once used chalkboards, or computers as a means for students to complete worksheets, but now with a digital platform. Obviously, deploying technology in this manner holds little potential for increased student learning.

Similarly, the assumption that giving students their own technology will increase ownership of learning and result in increased performance misses the point. Ownership of learning—which is, indeed, important if we want to significantly raise student performance—is embedded not in the technology itself but in the processes and strategies that allow students to take full advantage of technology and to exercise a measure of control over what, how, and where they will learn. If we operate within a system of legacy formats and traditional expectations—so that students are expected to comply in response to problems teachers develop and to complete tasks generated without consideration for their interests, current level of learning, and readiness for new learning challenges—it should not be a surprise that they do not necessarily feel ownership of learning.

It is not necessarily the case that technology lacks the potential to increase student learning. Examples of technology dramatically transforming and elevating the performance of other organizations and industries are many. However, the role technology has played in the transformation elsewhere is very different from what has happened in education. Technology was not considered a tool for efficiency alone or a means to better engage the client, although these elements often are by-products of the transformation. The transforming role of technology in other enterprises has been to facilitate and support deep rethinking and reorienting of the core work (think Amazon.com as compared to traditional bookstores). Technology made transformation possible. It was not seen as a tool to be integrated into work performed in much the same way it had been done in the past.

Moving from Transactional to Transformational Use of Technology

Realizing technology's promise will require rethinking and redesigning the intersection of teaching and learning to maximize the benefits it has to offer. In its current iteration, technology is primarily treated as a structural solution, driven by the notion that by changing structure we will change core behaviors. Technology holds the potential to support other efforts but does not offer high leverage for change by itself. As Rana Tamim and her colleagues (2011) conclude in their meta-analysis of 40 years of research on the impact of technology on student learning,

> It is arguable that it is aspects of the goals of instruction, pedagogy, teacher effectiveness, subject matter, age level, fidelity of technology implementation, and possibly other factors that may represent more powerful influences on effect sizes than the nature of the technology intervention. (p. 14)

The leverage in unleashing the power of technology lies in first developing a set of strategies that hold the potential to transform the way we think about and approach education and learning in the United States. We need to move beyond the transactional, lock-step approach that assumes 180 days of seat time equals one year's growth in learning. A system that is not designed or capable of responding to individual learning needs and readiness too often holds some students back while pushing others forward before they have learned core skills and strategies. We need a system that is customized to the point where engagement, agency, flexibility, and success are built in from the beginning rather than withheld until students fail, at which point we then attempt to remediate or otherwise intervene—a strategy that too often falls short and sends a message to learners that *they* are flawed.

When educators redesign teaching and learning to position the learner at the center and customize the instructional approach to meet learners' needs, we will be able to employ technology to support learning in ways that unleash potential; that ensure that learners are presented with tasks, content, and skill development that are relevant and appropriately calibrated to their learning needs; and that deliver on the promise of increasing student learning. However, this transformational—rather than transactional—approach must begin with the use of technology to support the correct instructional *strategy* rather than attempting to enhance an approach that lacks the leverage necessary to lift student performance beyond small increments and to significantly accelerate the pace of learning.

School Choice as a Structural Lever

Letting families and students choose where they will attend school has been promoted as a so-called silver bullet for improving education. The underlying assumption is that by promoting competition and a free market, the quality of education will improve. Stated another way, the problem with the current education system is that it enjoys too much of a monopoly and therefore has become unresponsive to pressures for change. A related assumption is that by expanding opportunities to create schools outside *the system*, innovation will flourish and performance will improve. The larger educational system will then respond by adopting key innovations in an attempt to better position itself to compete. Still another assumption has been that parents will be savvy in choosing schools and gravitate toward options that provide the best educational opportunities for their children.

Again, the promises of this approach have largely gone unrealized. After more than a decade of increased choice options, whether through charter schools, home schools, or voucher programs, the overall performance of the education system has barely changed. Equally significant, there is little evidence to support the argument that the institutions representing choice offer better learning outcomes overall. A 2009 study by the Center for Research on Education Outcomes concluded that charter schools as a whole produce no better results than the system they were supposed to surpass. Certainly many charter schools do better than many noncharter public schools, *and* many public schools outperform many charter schools; but when considered as a group, charter schools have not delivered significantly improved performance.

The picture is much the same when considered from the perspective of increased innovation. For the most part charter schools continue to educate students using the batch-processing approach of grouping students by age into classes taught by a single teacher with little regard to student readiness, preferred learning approach, or learning modalities. Other aspects of teaching and learning interactions continue to mirror traditional processes used in existing public or private schools. The consequence, unsurprisingly, is student learning results that are comparable to student performance in the noncharter schools.

A recent study of the Milwaukee school voucher program (Witte, Carlson, Cowen, Fleming, & Wolf, 2011) painted a similar picture of student learning outcomes. Students in voucher schools are not performing better than their counterparts in the public schools from which they came. Unfortunately, too many voucher schools have taken advantage of the lack of regulation to create revenue for founders at the expense of students and learning, even to the extent of creating "shells" masquerading as schools to collect public money. Until recently, voucher schools were not subject to any learning-related accountability, so comparing student performance was confined to graduation rates and other measures that often bear little meaningful relationship to high-quality learning. The lack of distinguishable performance among voucher schools compared to their public school counterparts further undermines the assumption that deregulation and choice alone will increase performance.

The assumption that parents will make choices based on educational quality also has not been universally supported. Although some parents actively and thoughtfully compare school performance and use it as the driving factor in the choice they make, many choose based on convenience and other factors not related to education, thus undermining the assumption that choice will influence quality.

The "bet" associated with choice as a school reform approach relies on a change in *structure* as a means to change behavior and resulting performance. However, this approach fails to focus on the core work of schools—teaching and learning—apparently assuming that the intersection between the two will somehow be changed and generate better outcomes as a result of a different structure. Although one can argue that structural changes may be necessary to facilitate and support changes at the core of the work, changing structure alone, as attractive and intuitive as it may seem, does not provide the leverage necessary to improve performance significantly, in a sustained manner, and at scale.

Seat Time as a Structural Lever

In a report on the effect of extended learning time in high schools, Hilary Pennington (2006) of the Center for American Progress describes the promise of longer school days and school years for students. In the report, she advocates that state governments consider experimenting with and implementing some "out of the box" extended-time strategies and encourages the creation of charter schools to adopt extended-time models. Secretary of Education Arne Duncan articulated his support for extended school time in a 2009 *Time* magazine article, stating, "I think the school day is too short, the school week is too short, and the school year is too short.... You look at all the creative schools that are getting dramatically better results. The common denominator of all of them is they're spending more time" (Stengel, 2009). Intuitively, this makes perfect sense. If some time in school results in some learning, shouldn't more time in school result in more learning?

Hundreds of schools have responded to this call. A recent article from the Center for American Progress (2010) reports that more than 650 schools in 36 states have engaged in extended-learning-time initiatives in recent years.

In their systematic, comprehensive review of the literature on extending the school day or the school year, Erika Patall, Harris Cooper, and Ashley Batts Allen (2010) sought to synthesize the research on the effect of extended school time on student learning. They articulate three conclusions: (1) there may be a small, positive effect on student learning associated with extended school time; (2) there is little risk in decreasing student achievement by extending school time; and (3) students at risk of failing may derive additional benefits from extended school time. However, Patall and her colleagues qualify their findings with the following explanation:

> How school time is used determines the effect of additional time on achievement. That is, the content and instructional strategies used in school are paramount to the success or failure of extending school time. It is only common sense that if additional school time is not used for instructional activities or if additional

instruction is of poor quality, it is unlikely to lead to achievement gains. In fact, if additional time is not used properly and school is experienced as boring or as punishment rather than as an enriching learning environment, it could lead to even undesirable student outcomes such as student fatigue or low motivation.... That is, the effectiveness of instruction might determine whether extended school time has positive, negative, or no effects on student outcomes. (p. 430)

These caveats are critically important. In other words, the leverage that structure provides is not a means to an end, but only provides a set of potentials that *may* be exercised to more effectively address other levers. We contend that this is true of all structural efforts. By their very nature structural changes are transactional. Assuming a change in structure will result in a change in student learning experience is *the* ubiquitous leveraging error. Educators need to pull other levers to fulfill the opportunity that any structural change may present.

Efforts to pull the structural lever of time are a response to the following question: How might achievement improve if we add more time to the school day? This query ignores the more powerful questions associated with strategy, standards, and self: How do we currently use instructional time (*strategy*)? How have we aligned expectations to ensure clarity of focus in our use of instructional time (*standards*)? To what extent is instructional time meaningful for all types of students (*self*)? Is our expectation for time-on-task that students are quiet and compliant, or that students are actively engaged in work they believe to be meaningful (*strategy, standard, self*)? These questions are at the core of the work we do as professional educators and at the core of student experience in the classroom. Until we've addressed, and maximized, our best collective efforts related to strategically addressing these questions, it is doubtful that additional learning time will result in significant improvement in student learning.

We've heard dozens of superintendents, principals, and teachers claim that structure must precede strategy: "We have plans to focus on technology and career skills by starting a new technology and career charter school," or "We can't increase collaboration until the board approves late start times," or "We can't use an instructional intervention program until the bus company changes its schedule." Changes in structure may require a lot of administrative effort, cause a stir in the community, and necessitate board action 18 months before the changes can even take place. However, we argue this type of thinking limits educators' capacity to focus on more accessible—and more important—levers. The standards of quality expected for student work, the instructional strategies used to teach to those standards, and the way we interact with students on a daily basis to inform their self-perceptions as learners—efforts in these areas can start well before any of these structural changes are put into place.

To be clear, we are not arguing that structure and resources are unimportant. Without clear and aligned structures and adequate resources, learning opportunities can diminish, and student achievement can suffer. Our argument is that having adequate or even abundant resources and well-formed and supportive structures will not, by itself, produce the leverage necessary to significantly increase and sustain high levels of student learning.

Structure: A Recap

In this chapter we've argued that using a change in structure as a lever for increased student learning rests on a false set of assumptions. Schools can engage in massive restructuring initiatives, yet student learning experiences can remain largely the same. Structural components are related to establishing conditions for learning, but standards, classroom strategies, and conceptualizations of self will need to be leveraged more effectively and efficiently than in the past for any restructuring effort to have a marked effect on student learning. Because structural change emphasizes clearly defined parameters and components that are easy for adults to define and discern but fail to significantly change the experience of the learner (for example, we used to have class for 51 minutes a day and now we have class for 54 minutes a day), changing school structure frequently results in a leverage error.

Connecting Structure to the Chapter Vignettes

Let's return briefly to the vignettes that opened this chapter. Each of them tells us something about the role structure often plays in school planning and the consequences of common misconceptions.

Reflections on Vignette 1: Traditional or Block Schedule? The principal in the first vignette is concerned with critical outcomes: student achievement and engagement. However, a schedule change does not ensure any effect on these outcomes. Considerable time, effort, and energy have been invested in addressing the structural change as *the* solution, and the structure-driven initiative has consumed two years of meetings, professional development, and resources that could have been invested in considering strategies to increase student engagement.

Over the years Jim has worked with a number of school districts that implemented block scheduling only to find that expected outcomes were not forthcoming. Unfortunately, the focus too often was on changing the time structure without corresponding changes in the ways students experienced learning and teachers used instructional strategies. As a result, learners were exposed to fewer classes per day, but not necessarily higher-quality learning experiences in those classes. Administrators became consumed with the logistics of the change in student scheduling. Teachers typically adjusted old lesson plans, activities, and approaches to the larger blocks of time but were unable to place students at the center of learning any more than with the previous schedule. Sadly, in some cases teachers not only did not change their instructional strategies but continued to present content to students as they had before the change and simply gave students study time during the remainder of the block—thus actually decreasing the amount of engagement in learning.

Reflections on Vignette 2: One-to-One Computing. In the second vignette, the district has addressed the structural issue of a technology gap in a manner that appears to have resolved an important equity issue. What is less clear is the extent to which the pilot schools are using different instructional strategies to leverage the new technology in a manner that will increase student learning. Furthermore, there is an assumption that access to technology results in higher achievement scores, but the standards for a 21st century learner are not necessarily synonymous with the standards aligned to a statewide achievement test.

We have seen a common pattern over the past decade in which investments in technology come with the expectation that new tools will increase learning as reflected in achievement test scores. The result typically has been an initial increase in student enthusiasm and engagement, followed by a return to previous patterns—*unless* teachers use instructional strategies that substantively integrate and leverage the new technology to change the experience of learners in ways that incorporate new learning skills, build independence, and extend learning opportunities. Narrowing the gap in access to technology is of little value unless educators tap the potential of the technology to support teaching and learning in ways that accelerate, deepen, and expand academic and other opportunities for students to increase their skills. Finally, technology can be a point of frustration rather than liberation for teachers and students unless adequate resources are available to ensure that the technology is widely accessible and highly reliable.

Connecting Structure to the Global Prosperity Academy

In the introduction to this book, the emphasis in the opening case about the Global Prosperity Academy was on structural, transactional changes: a smaller school, smaller class sizes, more computers, different report cards. The underlying assumption was that by making changes to the *school*, students would have a markedly different classroom experience that would result in improved learning. However, *a change in structure is not a change in strategy*. Changes in structure are prone to the leveraging error because the logistical components of structural change can consume time, energy, and resources that detract from the reason the change was put on the table in the first place.

Connecting Structure to the Kitchen Remodeling Analogy

When we think about remodeling, we are literally thinking about a process of taking existing structures and rearranging or changing them. Assuming access to basic structural components in the existing kitchen (such as a stove and a refrigerator), when we remodel we're really talking about using existing space differently or more efficiently. The central premise of the form, the function, and the materials used in the kitchen do not change; they are merely reconfigured. Although these technical changes in the structural components may result in a more aesthetically pleasing kitchen or a more convenient use of space, they do not improve the skills of the cook or the quality of the food. Too often when we engage in significant change efforts in schools, we reconfigure the structural components but do not transform the components that are most likely to improve the quality of student learning.

Doing Less, Doing More

To leverage structure effectively requires us to behave in certain ways. We must do less of some things—in essence, break ourselves of old habits and rid ourselves of persistent misconceptions; and we must do more of other things—namely, take actions and pursue strategies that are truly productive as we move toward our overarching goal of improved student performance. Figure 1.1 summarizes our recommendations for changes in behavior related to structure.

Figure 1.1 | Leveraging Structure

Do Less of This	Do More of This
• Assuming that a change in structure will result in a change in students' learning experiences	• Acknowledging that changes in structure merely create a set of opportunities to more effectively deploy practices designed to leverage standards, strategy, and conceptualizations of self
• Articulating changes in structure as the goal	• Clarifying that changes in structure are a means to the end of more effectively serving students' learning needs
• Waiting to change standards, strategy, or conceptualizations of self until after changes in structure have occurred	• Deploying strategies to actively leverage standards and productive conceptualizations of self as a matter of best practice that can occur in any classroom, on any day, at any time
• Assuming that a transactional change in policy or practice will result in a transformational change in teaching or learning	• Acknowledging the time and complexity of implementing transformational change
• Focusing on grand, district-level initiatives as the important agent in change	• Focusing on district- or building-level initiatives that acknowledge and support each teacher's classroom practice as the important agent of change

Reflecting on Structure: Questions to Ask on Monday Morning

- What drives the school structure? Tradition? Bus schedules? Adult convenience? Student learning needs?
- What amount or percentage of time do I or others in my school or district spend talking about structural changes as *the* primary lever associated with articulating concerns or creating new learning opportunities for students?
- When looking at agendas for board, faculty, team, and other meetings, to what extent do agenda items and meeting minutes deal with time, schedules, and logistics?
- To what extent is the implementation of specific structural changes discussed as *the goal* of initiatives in my school or district? Is adopting structural practices such as implementing a block schedule, adopting a new report card, or acquiring technology described as the goal or as a means to support more effective instructional practices?
- To what extent do we find ourselves waiting to address strategic opportunities or learning needs because we are waiting for structural components to fall into place (for example, we can't use new instructional strategies until new materials arrive; we can't spend more time talking about student performance on assessments until late-start collaborative time begins)?
- To what extent do we expect that structural change will result in a better learning experience for students or increased learning? How do we monitor the results of these structural changes in terms of their effect on students?
- If we are not achieving the results we hope to obtain under the current structure, are we attempting to address the problem or create better opportunities by reconfiguring more of the same structures and, by extension, largely maintaining each student's experience (through such things as longer class periods and summer school as a replication of the regular school year)?
- What is the relationship between the cost of this structural change—in terms of dollars, time, political chips, and other factors—and the expected results? Are there more direct, and more cost-effective, ways of addressing this issue?

Structure from the Students' Perspective

- How will the change in structure change students' learning experience?
- What connections will students be able to make between the changes in structure and new opportunities to improve their learning?
- How might students complete this prompt if the structural change is implemented effectively? *Before this change, I used to_____, but now I_____.*

Look at the tables in Appendix D related to status quo, transactional, and transformational planning questions and examine the questions associated with structure. What types of questions do you typically hear in your school or district related to structural changes? What types of questions do you typically ask?

Lever 2: Sample

Vignette 1: Single-Gender Classrooms

Upon returning from a conference that included a session on developmental differences between boys and girls, a superintendent convenes a study group to explore the possibility of gender-separate classrooms in science and mathematics. The study group reads a variety of sources that articulate different characteristics of boys and girls as learners and decides to recommend that the board move forward with a gender-separate initiative. The initiative becomes a somewhat contentious issue in the community, but the board unanimously supports the decision, stating that if the initiative might increase achievement, why not make the change? After the school has made significant efforts to redo the master schedule and engaged staff in a two-day training workshop, the new gender-separate groupings are implemented the following school year. The teachers find the training valuable and are eager to use the new instructional strategies at the start of the year.

Vignette 2: Ability Grouping in a High School Biology Course

A new schedule that includes late start times for students allows a small district's middle and high school science teachers to meet together monthly. The department chairs and the principals at each school are thrilled with this opportunity for collaboration. Placement of students in the high school honors biology course has long been a contentious issue, with about 20 percent of freshmen placed in the class each year. Of these students, about 10 percent earn a *C* or lower. The middle and high school teams decide to make criteria for biology placement their top priority for how they will use their collaborative time. They spend the year analyzing the test scores and learning profiles of the students who have been misplaced into the honors class in years past. They establish a new set of cut scores and purchase a screening assessment to be administered to all 8th grade students. The following year, even fewer students are admitted into the honors class, but about the same percentage earn a *C* or lower.

Vignette 3: Ability Grouping in an Elementary Gifted and Talented Program

Parents in a high-achieving suburban district place a high level of importance on small class size and their children's access to the district's gifted and talented program. By investing in additional classroom teachers, the district is able to support class sizes of about 21 students. Unfortunately, this leaves enough resources for only one gifted and talented (GT) teacher in each building. For several years the district has used a decision tree of clear qualification criteria to ensure that the students with the strongest profiles can access the GT teacher. Each year, identified students do a literature circle, a writing activity, and a special project with the GT teacher. Despite these efforts, the GT teachers spend a significant amount of time addressing concerns from parents of students who have been excluded from the program, as well as from parents whose students have been identified for the program but want more services.

Vignette 4: Multi-age Classes

Three 2nd and 3rd grade teachers approach their principal with a request to move from age-based classroom grouping to mixed-age combinations of 2nd and 3rd graders in the same number of classes. The teachers argue that some 2nd grade students are capable of moving more quickly than the 2nd grade curriculum allows and could benefit from working with 3rd graders in some areas and on some skills. Meanwhile, some 3rd grade students need more time to master 2nd grade standards. In a multi-age classroom, these students could receive the support they need and continue to build their learning without the negative outcomes closely associated with grade retention. The teachers volunteer to rework the 2nd and 3rd grade curricula so that all students will be at least as advanced at the end of 3rd grade as most students are now, but with more time and flexibility to achieve success.

Sample: Definition, Misconception, and Opportunity

Definition: *Sample is the grouping of students in any classroom, program, or learning opportunity at any given time.*

Schools typically make decisions about which groups of students should be assigned to certain classrooms based on students' identified need for challenge or support. This could include access to support programs or to advanced classes. It also includes programs that schedule students based on specific attributes such as special education needs, career tracks, or gender. The most widely applied sampling strategy is grouping students by age, or as author and education advisor Sir Ken Robinson asserts, "date of manufacture" (Robinson, 2010). Anyone who has been a parent, sibling, or teacher understands that children learn in different ways and at different rates. Yet grouping students by age works against attempts to personalize learning in response to student needs. In his book *Outliers*, Malcolm Gladwell (2008) creates a compelling argument that using arbitrary dates to decide children's access to developmental experiences presents opportunities for some and disadvantages for others, creating lifelong trajectories that consistently accelerate or inhibit learning.

Misconception: *Placing students in the course, track, or level that has been designated for them will ensure their learning needs are addressed.*

At its worst, changing the sample is merely a process of reshuffling students into different classrooms, especially when instructional strategies and curricular opportunities are not differentiated or personalized in a meaningful way. In some schools, the sample of students is manipulated so some students can proceed at a slower pace if they need greater support or a faster pace if they need greater challenge. However, this approach provides only limited potential to maximize student learning (Loveless, 2013). In fact, for many students this practice sends a damaging and erroneous message that they are not capable of learning at higher levels (Dornbusch, 1994).

Opportunity: *Align high standards with appropriate strategies.*

Changing the sample of students in a school or classroom serves as an effective lever for student learning only if it allows for the deployment of more effective instructional practices that are designed to address the specific learning needs of that group of students. Too often, grouping practices have the detrimental effect of placing low expectations on learners. If student sampling is used, several conditions should be in place. Students should have (1) access to effective, research-based learning experiences that could not be delivered in a heterogeneous setting; (2) fluid opportunities to move from one level of challenge or support to another; and (3) access to good learning models and the support necessary to achieve at high levels.

The Lure of Changing the Sample

The idea seems very intuitive: grouping students with similar profiles together will enable them to learn more. Although this notion sounds self-evident, it is not. In fact, landmark studies (such as the study that reported the Pygmalion effect, Rosenthal & Jacobson, 1968) and Supreme Court decisions (including *Brown v. Board of Education*) have fervently argued just the opposite.

A provocative essential question frames hundreds of years of discussion and debate about sampling practices in U.S. schools: Whom do our schools serve, and where should those students go in order to be best served? To trace the history of this question is to trace the grand narratives of American history. This question was at the heart of discussion and debate as the nation's education system evolved from the rural one-room schoolhouse to the comprehensive system of rural, suburban, and urban elementary, middle, and high schools that exists today. It was at the heart of landmark legal battles as the United States emerged from the Civil War and progressed through the civil rights movement. It was at the heart of the evolution of a society from one that prepared girls to become secretaries, elementary teachers, or nurses to one in which women outnumber men on college campuses. It was at the heart of some of the most important Supreme Court decisions of the 20th century. And it is at the heart of debates about how equality and access are connected to race and class through public, private, choice, and charter schools.

In this chapter we consider just a few examples of how schools use sampling procedures—making decisions about which kids should be in which classrooms based on specific characteristics and attributes—in an attempt to improve efficiencies for teachers and outcomes for students. We examine ability grouping, single-gender classrooms, and retention and acceleration practices and place those components into a broader context through the Five-Lever Framework.

Ability Grouping

Despite ubiquitous research arguing against practices that use sampling in an attempt to improve student learning, such practices persist. In a report titled "The Resurgence of Ability Grouping and Persistence of Tracking," Tom Loveless (2013) used data from the National Assessment of Educational Progress to document the resurgence of grouping in 4th grade reading. According to Loveless, in 1961 about 80 percent of elementary schools used ability grouping to sort students. By 1998, that percentage had fallen to 28 percent. Between 1998 and 2009, however, that number steadily increased to 71 percent. Similar trends are noted in 4th grade math, as well as in 8th grade math and reading. What is most troubling about this trend is the author's citation of sources that support claims that grouping practices are discriminatory, represent significant underlying equity issues, and provide little benefit for students in higher groups and have a detrimental effect on learning for those in the lower groups.

Grouping practices are deeply embedded in the structure of schools. Schools' clustering of students by age groups is simply accepted as how schools are supposed to be organized. Within these age-group clusters, students are sometimes sampled by characteristics such as ability (students who require more challenge or support), interest (as in specialty programs or career clusters), or labeled status (special education, gifted and talented).

Although sorting and sampling students occurs in a number of ways, ability grouping and tracking are the most dominant. Ability grouping is the practice of moving students into different classes based on their current achievement profile in a specific domain. When ability grouping is used across the majority of the school day, it is called *tracking*. Tracking occurs when students' entire schedules are sorted into academic clusters made up of honors, college prep, general education, or vocational education courses, or clusters identified by other demarcations. Ability grouping differs from tracking in that ability grouping tends to place students on a course-by-course basis rather than position them for access to an entire slate of courses. Finally, in-class ability grouping typically involves clustering a small group of students for a specific subject or for a specific learning sequence within that subject. For example, students in an elementary reading class may be placed into a "high" or a "low" reading group. All of these practices represent efforts to manipulate the sample of students in order to better address their learning needs.

Pros and Cons

As noted, proponents of ability grouping argue that by clustering students with similar learning profiles, teachers can more easily address the students' learning needs. Opponents argue that grouping often has a negative effect on students' perception of their ability to learn or places them in a learning environment that deprives them of the opportunity to learn grade-level curricula. With the best of intentions, ability grouping represents educators' efforts to ensure that every child—regardless of race, gender, or class—has access to a set of learning experiences that balance the challenge and support required to maximize that child's learning. At its worst, ability grouping represents educators' implicit acceptance of the idea that some groups of students are worthy of more authentic and rigorous learning experiences that will be taught at a faster pace, whereas others are merely buying time until they drop out or are "given" a diploma.

Although ability grouping is typical in U.S. and British schools, Asian countries such as Japan use grouping strategies at a dramatically lower rate. In fact, analysis of international comparisons (Clarke & Clarke, 2008) shows that countries that are more likely to expose all students to rigorous curricula and that rely less on ability grouping tend to outperform those that rely more heavily on stratification of learning experiences through sampling.

Research on Ability Grouping

In a best-evidence synthesis of 43 studies on ability grouping in elementary schools, Robert Slavin (1987) found that grouping students into different classes based on their ability had no effect on their learning. With an overall effect size of 0.00, the practice literally made no difference. However, within-class, small-scale, flexible grouping practices in some specific classes did have a positive effect on student learning. Specifically, Slavin concluded that students should spend the majority of the day with their heterogeneous class, grouped as necessary in only a few core academic subjects to allow for targeted instruction in specific reading or mathematics skills. Finally, he concluded that students should be reassessed frequently to ensure that placements are fluid and driven by student learning needs.

More recently, in her literature review tracing the history and semantics of ability grouping across the 20th century, Jo Worthy (2010) identified a number of consistent themes across the literature. These themes include the following:

- Students in higher-track classes were more likely to be taught by more experienced, higher-credentialed teachers.
- Higher-track classes were more likely to be fast-paced and engaging.
- Lower-track classes were more likely to focus on didactic, rote tasks and test preparation.
- Teachers who work with students in both tracks were more likely to describe higher-track students using positive terms and articulated higher-order learning goals for these students. Conversely, these teachers were more likely to describe lower-track students using negative terms and articulated goals related to behavior and conforming to rules and norms rather than learning.
- Students in lower tracks were taught curriculum at a much slower rate, thereby exacerbating, rather than closing, achievement gaps.

Given these findings, it is not surprising that ability grouping is such a contentious issue for parents, educators, and advocates for children who are grouped into lower tracks.

Overall, the various sampling procedures seem to have little effect on improving student learning. In his synthesis of meta-analyses, John Hattie (2009) found little to no meaningful effects for various grouping processes. Hattie's synthesis of more than 300 studies of tracking found little to no effect on student learning, with only slight gains for high- and low-track students and a negative effect on students in the middle track. As Hattie concludes, "No one profits" (p. 90). Hattie reached similar conclusions in his analysis of more than 90 studies that considered the effect of multi-age classrooms. Multi-age classrooms are formed when two or more grades are combined into a single classroom. Hattie found that the effect on student learning across the synthesis of studies on multi-age classrooms was near zero. Similarly, small to no effects were found for various within-class grouping practices. In reference to multi-age classes, Hattie hypothesizes why grouping practices have such a small effect on student learning:

> It is likely that teachers teach in a similar way regardless of the distribution of age range in the class, and the multi-grade classes are often split by age for grouping. There is a deeply embedded grammar of teaching that appears to remain the same regardless of these structural changes in classes. Hence, it is not surprising that there are close to zero findings. (p. 93)

From the lens of the Five-Lever Framework, we are not surprised by these findings. In fact, Hattie's conclusions about multi-age classes sound remarkably like Patall, Cooper, and Allen's findings (2010; see Chapter 1) in their analysis of structural changes that extend the school day. Changes in sampling of students can merely be a facade for meaningful change. The kitchen has been remodeled, but the chef's skills and the ingredients have remained the same. From the perspective of the students, the food still tastes the same. The status quo of curriculum, instruction, and assessment has been maintained; it is merely being delivered in a different context. The leverage provided by sampling students based on ability is not a means to an end; it merely provides a set of potential conditions that *may* be exercised to more effectively address other levers.

Single-Gender Classrooms

In 2006 the U.S. Department of Education rescinded some specific components of the Title IX prohibition against single-sex classrooms. Under the new guidelines, single-sex classes are permissible as long as participation is voluntary, students have an equal coeducational option, and the school believes the different gender groupings will produce better academic achievement.

Dr. Leonard Sax has been on the leading edge of the argument that schools need to do a better job tending to differences between boys and girls. Sax, a physician and executive director of the National Association for Choice (formerly the National Association for Single-Sex Public Education), has written numerous articles and books on gender differences as related to classroom learning. Recent titles by Sax include *Girls on the Edge: The Four*

Factors Driving the New Crisis for Girls (2010) and *Boys Adrift: The Five Factors Driving the Growing Epidemic of Unmotivated Boys and Underachieving Young Men* (2007). In these books, Sax combines anecdotes and research to build the argument that by ignoring gender differences, educators have neglected to provide responsive education environments for boys and girls. Sax advocates for the use of specific approaches and strategies that are aligned to cognitive differences in how boys and girls are wired. These approaches range from emphasizing competition for boys and cooperation for girls, to using a direct tone of voice to challenge boys versus using a calm tone of voice with girls in order to communicate affirmation and acceptance (Sax, 2007). Many schools have heeded his call by sampling boys and girls into different classes. In 2002 there were only 11 public schools with gender-separate classes, but by the end of the decade there were more than 550 (Holthouse, 2010).

Diane Halpern of Claremont McKenna University disagrees with Sax's premise that there are broad, cognitive differences between boys and girls. Furthermore, she believes grouping students by gender does harm to kids. In a 2011 article in *Science* titled "The Pseudoscience of Single-Sex Schooling," Halpern and her colleagues argue not only that there is little evidence that single-sex classrooms improve student learning but that such classrooms increase gender stereotypes and validate a system of institutional sexism. According to Halpern and her colleagues,

> Although excellent public single-sex schools clearly exist, there is no empirical evidence that their success stems from their single-sex organization, as opposed to the quality of the student body, demanding curricula, and many other features also known to promote achievement at coeducational schools. (p. 1706)

A 2005 study from the U.S. Department of Education supports Halpern and her colleagues' assertion that on average, single-sex classrooms demonstrate no significant differences in student achievement as compared to heterogeneous classrooms.

Of even greater concern is the effect of single-sex classrooms on students' and teachers' perceptions of gender differences, furthering of stereotypes, and the elevation of gender as the single most important factor in defining a child's dispositions, interests, and needs. These concerns highlight a key challenge of sampling students in efforts to improve their learning. Although the sampling processes *may* create the potential for teachers to deliver instruction and engage students in more meaningful ways, the process itself can have a negative effect on students' self-systems, perpetuating stereotypes or enabling students' beliefs about their ability or inadequacy to become self-fulfilling prophecies (Dweck, 2000; Steele, Spencer, & Aronson, 2002).

Retention and Acceleration

Two sampling processes *do* have significant effects—among the strongest we've seen in both research and practice—on student learning: retention and acceleration. What is interesting is that these effects are profoundly negative for retention and profoundly strong for acceleration.

Retention is one of the few consistently used "innovations" of educational practice that actually has a negative effect on student learning. As Hattie (2009) states, a review of the research on retention yields almost no studies with a positive effect. Across more than 200 studies on retention, Hattie found a negative effect on academic achievement in every academic area, as well as negative effects on attendance. Furthermore, these negative effects tend to compound year over year, resulting in an increased chance of falling so far behind and becoming so disillusioned that retained students are twice as likely to drop out of school. Finally, citing two different studies (Cosden, Zimmer, & Tuss, 1993; Meisels & Liaw, 1993), Hattie states that there are inequities in how retention is used, based on race. African American and Hispanic students are four times as likely to be retained as their white peers—even when levels of academic achievement are the same (p. 98). In the end, "the preponderance of evidence argues that students who repeat a grade are no better off, and are sometimes worse off, than if they had been promoted with their classmates" (David, 2008, p. 84).

At the other end of the spectrum are the effects of acceleration for high-achieving students. Many advocates for gifted students argue that gifted students are the least well-served students in schools (Farkas, Duffett, & Loveless, 2008). In a No Child Left Behind era focused on ensuring that there are no low-achievers in America's schools, many schools and districts have scaled back on specialists who are responsible for addressing the learning needs of students who require challenge beyond grade-level curricula. In a review of two meta-analyses comprising nearly 40 studies, Hattie (2009) reports a strong effect—nearly a full standard deviation of achievement—among students who were accelerated into a higher grade. Furthermore, the effects of acceleration were nearly twice as large as the effects of enrichment programs or within-class grouping practices for gifted students. Remarkably, grade acceleration requires no additional structural resources. It merely requires a process to identify and place the small number of students in each school for whom grade acceleration might be most appropriate. Although some individuals are resistant to considering acceleration because of the possibility of negative social effects on children, Hattie reports a positive effect on gifted students' social needs and a negative effect on social needs when these students are *not* accelerated.

From the lens of the five levers, avoiding retention as a means of intervention for students who struggle and embracing acceleration for extremely high-achieving students makes a lot of sense. For students who fail, it should be apparent that the current classroom practices are not a match with their learning needs. These students are likely experiencing a significant gap between their interests, skills, and assets, on the one hand, and what is provided in the classroom, on the other. To merely return to the same classroom (or a similar classroom), where the same curriculum is delivered once again in a manner that uses the same instructional strategies, is a bit like realizing the milk in your refrigerator is spoiled but placing it back in the refrigerator and trying it again a few days later. Why should we be surprised when simply maintaining the status quo provides similar results?

At the other end of the spectrum, how do we become aware of students who may require additional challenge through grade acceleration? Typically these are students who are capable of performing exceptionally well on standardized tests and complete coursework and homework easily. In other words, these are students whose strengths and learning needs *are well aligned to the structures and strategies* that are currently being used. The key variable that has not been particularly well aligned in these students' journey through school is that the practice of sampling students by age has prevented them from accessing the level of challenge they require through more rigorous standards. Grade (or subject) acceleration allows for a single change in sample to address this need. This can be done in a manner that does not create a negative conceptualization of self for the student being accelerated, nor is it a losing situation for those who are not accelerated (Rogers, 2002).

Sample: A Recap

Too often sampling is merely a specific type of structural, transactional exchange whereby students are grouped into clusters based on a common attribute (such as gender or reading achievement scores) and then exposed to many of the same instructional strategies that had been used in their earlier classroom environment. Although the classroom context may change, the student's learning experience remains largely unchanged. Furthermore, many sampling processes define clusters of students based on a set of attributes that have been perceived to be liabilities rather than assets. This can result in a set of unintended consequences that create winners (those whose learning needs are already well aligned with what the system provides) and losers (those whose learning needs are not as well served). Furthermore, some sampling processes rest on the premise that more effective instructional strategies or strategic use of standards can occur only after new sampling processes have been put into place. When using sample as a lever to accelerate student learning, it is critically important that educators consider the time, effort, and energy they spend on student placement processes to be good investments only if the result is the opportunity to link standards and strategies more effectively to each student's specific learning needs.

Connecting Sampling to the Chapter Vignettes

The vignettes at the start of this chapter presented various scenarios highlighting the role that sample may play in school planning related to change. Three of them illustrate common misperceptions about sample, whereas one demonstrates a thoughtful approach to using sample as a lever for change—but even in that case, those involved need to consider some important questions to ensure that they gain the intended leverage advantage.

Reflections on Vignette 1: Single-Gender Classrooms. Two premises in this vignette are relevant from a five-levers perspective: (1) *if* there are differences in how boys and girls learn, *then* they need to be placed in different classes to learn most effectively; and (2) *if* there are instructional strategies that may be more effective for each gender, *then* students need to be placed in different classes for teachers to use those strategies. Both of these premises are false. This example attempts to leverage sample (grouping) and structure (the master schedule) as the means to address issues of students' perceptions of themselves as learners (as related to gender) and the use of effective instructional strategies (again, as related to gender). Could the instructional strategies taught in the workshop have been deployed without changing the sample and structure? Have teachers had the opportunity to develop expertise in the use of those strategies? These are critical questions that must be addressed to avoid the leveraging error of changing sample when changing the use of instructional strategies might have been not only more efficient, but more effective.

Reflections on Vignette 2: Ability Grouping in a High School Biology Course. Rather than consider ways to build the capacity to use even more effective instructional strategies, the efforts in the ability grouping for a high school biology course assume that teachers' capacity to teach and students' capacity to learn are fixed characteristics. The focus in this vignette is on raising the standard for access to ensure that only the sample that is guaranteed success in the course *as currently structured* will be admitted. Instead of using the new collaborative time to consider how teaching and learning might be transformed through changes in curriculum, instruction, and assessment that would more mindfully connect strategies and students to standards, the team has chosen to maintain the status quo and focus on a transactional change in the gatekeeping process.

Reflections on Vignette 3: Ability Grouping in an Elementary Gifted and Talented Program. Sampling limitations are at play in this vignette about a program for gifted and talented students. At first, the limitation appears to be limited access to GT enrichment opportunities. The assumption seems to be that *if* students demonstrate characteristics of a gifted learner, *then* their needs must be met by working directly with a GT teacher who is also working with other gifted students at that time. What if the GT teacher worked to build the capacity of *all* teachers to better leverage standards and strategies to address the needs of gifted learners? For a child with exceptional learning needs—whether those needs are for additional challenge or additional support—there is little leverage in a system that allows for targeted instructional opportunities to occur during only 5 or 10 percent of each student's total instructional time during the school year. If the child has a truly exceptional need for additional challenge, then perhaps acceleration—one of the few sampling practices with a consistent track record of improving student achievement—should be pursued. If that is not the case, an emphasis on improving the repertoire of responsive instructional strategies of those teachers with whom that student will spend the majority of the school day will provide more consistent opportunities to support learning.

Reflections on Vignette 4: Multi-age Classes. The intent, strategies, and anticipated outcomes associated with the teachers' advocacy for multi-age classes appear to be well aligned. The teachers are committed to transforming their professional practice in an attempt to transform student learning. Their premise for the change is strong; it starts with a desire to be responsive to student learning needs. They see the capacity in each student and are interested in using time as a flexible, rather than a fixed, variable to support student learning. However, the same types of questions referenced in the reflections on the single-gender classroom need to be addressed in this case as well: How is assessment currently used to guide each teacher's and student's efforts to link standards and strategy? What classroom strategies that support leveraging a multi-age classroom could be deployed without making the structural change? We've found that by asking these types of questions—and providing teachers the time to address and then act on them—teams can be remarkably adept at decoupling sampling from strategy, thereby avoiding a leveraging error. Teachers are empowered when they understand that the decisions they make about curriculum, instruction, and assessment can provide more powerful leverage to influence student learning than changes in sampling or strategy that typically require administrative, board, or even state department of education approval. This does not mean that the sampling change isn't warranted or shouldn't be tried at any point. If warranted, the change in sample will most likely result in success when teachers have thoroughly explored and implemented some of the strategies most likely to provide the leverage advantage necessary to obtain the desired outcomes. If teachers find they are bumping up against limitations that prevent them from further implementation of strategies that are even more transformational, the change in sampling may very well be required to obtain the leverage advantage.

Connecting Sampling to the Global Prosperity Academy

The case of the Global Prosperity Academy, presented in the introduction to this book, described several ways that the school hoped to leverage sampling to improve student learning. The school sought to attract students with a specific interest in curricula aligned to the school's mission. Furthermore, the school drew from within that sample to assign students to a different sequence of courses. The underlying assumption was that if the sample of students who selected the school was interested in a particular kind of curriculum, that element alone would lead them to be more motivated to learn the curriculum. A second assumption was that any within-group differences among students at the school could be best met by creating different tracks. These tracks resulted in the unintended consequence of creating factions within the school.

In our experience, attempts to improve learning by focusing on changing the sample of students often fall short because of the core assumption that grouping students based on a few characteristics is enough to improve learning. This kind of thinking risks ignoring myriad other characteristics that the students do not share but which still affect learning. For many students, the characteristic or characteristics on which the grouping is based may be a minor or incidental element when it comes to their learning. Even worse, they may be grouped by a set of characteristics that have been deemed to be liabilities. They would often be better served in an environment where their characteristics as learners are viewed and leveraged holistically, so that the instruction they experience taps their greatest strengths and strongest interests and addresses their most significant learning needs. This type of learning environment can be created in a variety of contexts and does not demand an explicit sampling approach.

Connecting Sampling to the Kitchen Remodeling Analogy

In our kitchen remodeling analogy, the leveraging error—assuming that changing the context where cooking occurs would improve the taste of food prepared in the space—left the family disappointed. Even though in the kitchen analogy the outcome seems obvious, school leaders often introduce different student grouping configurations without making significant changes to learning content, instructional strategies, or relationships between students and their learning and expect different learning results. The absence of change to the outcome is no less predictable in the classroom. Too often, students who find themselves subjected to new grouping practices often share the observation offered by the child in the kitchen: there is not a meaningful change in the resulting experience.

Doing Less, Doing More

To get the most benefit from using sample as a lever, we may need to reconsider some aspects of how we think and behave. Figure 2.1 summarizes the kinds of behaviors we should do less of, and those we should do more of, if we want to use sample as an effective lever for improving student learning.

Figure 2.1 | Leveraging Sample

Do Less of This	Do More of This
• Assuming that because kids are grouped differently, their instructional needs are being met more effectively	• Building capacity to differentiate instructional strategies for all students
• Investing time and energy pursuing perfect student placement systems	• Investing time and energy in ensuring that regardless of placement, each student experiences an appropriate balance of challenge and support
• Assuming that kids aren't aware of, and don't internalize, the stigma of being placed in a group that is perceived to be "lower and slower"	• Considering and responding to the effect of grouping practices on each student's self-perception as a learner, including how students can internalize perceptions of race, poverty, ethnicity, and gender as liabilities
• Providing limited access to learning experiences that target students' individual needs (e.g., a two-week gifted and talented pullout session, a weekly math support session) and ignoring those needs when students aren't in those clustered groups	• Ensuring that through differentiated curriculum and instruction, students have access to an appropriate balance of challenge and support in the classrooms where they spend the majority of their time
• Using rigid, fixed grouping practices that create tracks or clusters of low- and high-achieving students	• Using flexible grouping and skill-based, unit-level pre-assessments to differentiate units of instruction based on specific learning needs

Reflecting on Sample: Questions to Ask on Monday Morning

- What drives grouping practices in our school or school district? Tradition? Adult convenience? Assumptions about students' strengths and needs? Student learning needs?
- What is the amount or percentage of time I or others in my school or district spend talking about grouping changes as *the* primary lever associated with articulating concerns or creating new learning opportunities for students? How might these resources be redirected to be more productive?
- When looking at agendas for board, faculty, team, and other meetings, to what extent do agenda items and meeting minutes deal with processes and criteria related to placing students in different programs versus classroom processes and strategies that can best meet the needs of these learners?
- How are staffing decisions linked to sampling? What is the general profile (experience, credentials) of individuals who work with learners who need greater support?
- Do learners who need greater challenge or support experience instructional strategies designed specifically to match their different needs?
- To what extent is the implementation of specific grouping practices discussed as *the goal* of initiatives in our school or district? Are practices that manipulate the sample, such as new support programs or additional levels of classes or tracks, described as *the* goal or a means to a different end? How might we shift the focus to make a greater difference for learners?
- To what extent are student groups described as *desirable* ("higher-achieving," "higher-compliance," and so on) as compared to *undesirable* ("lower-achieving," "lower-compliance") when we are considering placement decisions?
- What are the underlying equity issues related to our grouping practices? Do grouping processes result in segregation by gender? Race? Socioeconomic status?
- To what extent are needs and interests of students in different groupings cast as assets ("creative," "inquisitive") or liabilities ("noncompliant," "questions authority")?

- To what extent do we find ourselves waiting to address strategic opportunities or learning needs because we are waiting for new sampling procedures to be put into place (for example, we can't meet the learning needs of a particular group of students until the new course is added or the new program is implemented)?
- To what extent do we find teachers waiting to address student learning needs, or absolving themselves from addressing student learning needs, because there is a different adult/program/service in the school that holds a more primary obligation to tend to that student (as indicated by statements such as "He's one of [special education teacher] Ms. Lopez's kids")?
- To what extent do we expect that changing the sample will result in a better learning experience for students or increased learning? How do we monitor the results in terms of the effect of the change on students?
- If we are not achieving the results we hope to obtain under the current sampling procedures, do we attempt to address the problem or create better opportunities by regrouping students for a similar learning experience (for example, similar curriculum, instruction, and assessment strategies but deployed at a slower or faster pace)?
- What is the relationship between the cost of this sampling change— in terms of dollars, time, political chips, and other factors—and the expected results? Are there more direct, and more cost-effective, ways of addressing this issue?

Questions on Sample from the Students' Perspective

- How will a change in sampling change each student's learning experience?
- How will the resampling of students affect their perceptions of themselves as learners? To what extent might these groupings affirm perceptions of abilities as fixed ("I am good at science" or "I am bad at math") rather than developmental ("If I work hard, I can get better at this" or "I just haven't found the best way to learn this yet")?
- How might sampling decisions create groups among students (in-groups, out-groups, "smart" groups, "dumb" groups), and what will be done to deal with perceptions or factions that may be harmful to individual learners? To school culture?

- How might students complete this prompt if the sampling change is implemented effectively? *Before this change, I used to _____, but now I _____.*

Look at the tables in Appendix D related to status quo, transactional, and transformational planning questions and examine the questions associated with sample. What types of questions do you typically hear in your school or district when you are discussing changes in sample? What types of questions do you typically ask?

Lever 3: Standards

Vignette 1: Alignment and Binders

A few months after new state standards are introduced, teachers convene in the cafeteria for a professional development day. The curriculum director passes out copies of the existing curriculum-alignment documents for the various grade levels and subject areas to the respective teams of teachers. Next the curriculum director passes out copies of the new standards. "Here's what I need you to do," announces the director. "See where the old standards are on the curriculum documents? Cross those out and put in the new standard that you think is most similar to the old standard." The following week, the curriculum director tells the administrative team and the school board that the curriculum has been aligned to the new standards.

Vignette 2: If a Few Are Good, More Must Be Better

Noted for having high expectations in his middle school history classes, Mr. Smith tells parents during orientation night that whereas some teachers have a 93 percent cutoff for an *A*, his cutoff is 94 percent. Furthermore, he expects his students to memorize the names of *all* of the states and capitals, *all* of the presidents, and *all* of the vice presidents.

Vignette 3: Prioritizing for a Purpose

Faced with the challenge of implementing new standards, a regional group of curriculum directors convenes nearly 50 teachers and curriculum specialists from various districts, schools, and grade levels for a day-long overview of the form and function of the standards. At the end of the day the group is given the following charge, to be completed in the next three sessions: *At each grade level, rank the standards in order of importance for ensuring students are prepared to be successful at the next level. Given this ranking, what are the implications for prioritizing efforts related to the development of quality assessment? Curriculum? Instruction?*

Vignette 4: Standards Through Students' Eyes

Both nervous and excited, Shawna opens her portfolio and explains to her parents and her teacher how three work samples from the previous year demonstrate growth in her ability to solve multistep word problems in math. As she explains the differences in the work samples ("At the beginning of the year _____, but now I know that _____. Next year I am going to learn how to _____"), the adults smile at each other and nod. "How exciting," says her teacher. "That is exactly what you are going to learn how to do next year in 5th grade!"

Definition, Misconception, and Opportunity

Definition: *Standards are the expectations for student learning.*

Standards are the specifically articulated components related to the rigor, richness, and levels of expectations for student mastery of content knowledge and skills.

Misconception: *More of everything is a way to raise standards for learning.*

Falling victim to the "more is better" mantra of schooling is easy. It seems intuitive that more homework, more math problems, longer essays, longer tests, and higher grading scales result in a more rigorous environment, which results in more learning. Unfortunately, the rush to cover content, increase learning time, and otherwise raise the bar for success is more often an impediment to student learning than a lever to significantly increase student performance (Gardner, 1991). This superficial, transactional approach fails to honor the depth and intentionality required to implement standards in a meaningful way.

Opportunity: *Use standards strategically to clarify teaching and learning goals in a manner that results in new ways of nurturing and assessing learning.*

By prioritizing standards based on their potential to affect student learning across disciplines and using formative assessments that break standards into small, manageable pieces, standards can be a powerful lever to improve student learning. However, they must be accompanied by aligned student supports and scaffolding to allow students to meet or exceed the standards. Ultimately, students—not only teachers—must be able to use standards to guide efforts toward achievement and mastery. Implementation of new standards must be done in a manner that ensures that they result in different experiences for students; curriculum, instruction, assessment, and rubrics should look different in a classroom where a new set of standards is being used to guide student learning.

The Transformational Potential of Standards

The concept of standards is not unique to the field of education. Name a process that involves a group of people, and it undoubtedly includes standards that need to be met. In manufacturing, health care, business, and education, standards are articulated by agencies or organizations to guide the attention and efforts of professionals within those fields. Sometimes these are standards established by watchdog groups such as the Better Business Bureau, professional organizations such as the American Medical Association, or federal agencies such as the Office of Safety and Health Administration. Standards matter profoundly because they have the potential to transform entire areas of society and improve the quality of life for entire countries. If you've read Upton Sinclair's classic novel *The Jungle*, you know that American meat-processing plants circa 1900 looked radically different than they do today. Remarkable changes have been made to ensure the processes used result in a safer product. Many of these differences are related to changes in technology. However, many of these changes in technology are the outcome of innovation and invention that occurred *as a result* of efforts to meet more rigorous government standards for cleanliness and safety.

Often, when new standards are put in place, the skills, processes, or technologies required to meet those standards haven't been developed yet. To transcend the status quo, the affected field needs to not merely restructure a few parts of the process but transform how work is done in the field to rise to the new, higher expectations for quality performance.

An example of how standards can stretch an entire field to new levels of innovation to achieve outcomes that were once deemed impossible is fuel efficiency standards for automobiles. In 1975 the typical American automobile could go 13.5 miles per gallon of gasoline (Pew, 2011). Given a set of global issues that caused Congress to see fuel efficiency as a factor that was central to the nation's economic well-being, legislation was passed to double the standards for fuel efficiency in 10 years. At the time, the technology to meet these standards on a national scale did not exist. Professionals in the field—chemists, engineers, physicists—used their expertise to change their approach to designing and producing automobiles. This was not a *transactional* process of describing how portions of their current processes were correlated to the development and design of a fleet of automobiles that would meet the new standards. This was a *transformational* process of reconceptualizing their work. Starting with the new efficiency standards and working backward, they needed to specifically address and intentionally change myriad chemical and physical processes associated with the design and production of automobiles. Between 1975 and 1985, mileage for automobiles more than doubled, from 13.5 miles per gallon to 27.5 miles per gallon. The components that made this possible—participation of individuals with specialized professional expertise and a reconceptualization of the design process that started with key outcomes as the premise for the work—are the same accelerating or limiting factors at play in educators' efforts to leverage standards to improve student learning.

Earlier in this book, we pointed out that the leverage error most associated with *structure* or *sample* is pulling the wrong lever. For example, time, effort, and resources are spent changing the school structure when the use of more effective instructional strategies could have yielded better results. In contrast, it would be difficult for a school to pay too much attention to standards. As Tom Guskey and Lee Ann Jung (2013) state, standards "define the learning expectations or goals that educators strive to have students attain. As such, standards provide the foundation for every school's curriculum and instructional program" (p. 2). Standards can be extremely high-leverage components of the education system. The challenge of leveraging standards is in *how* they are used. Standards can be used in a transactional manner that maintains the status quo of student experience and achievement in schools, or they can be leveraged in a manner that transforms the roles of teachers and learners.

Conceptualizations of Standards over Time

The history, or etymology, of words helps us understand their meaning. The meaning of the word *standard* has evolved over time, but each meaning continues to influence how we use the word today. Originally, *standard* referred to large flags or markers on a path along a route. Before maps and long before GPS, standards could be placed along a route between two points to help guide travelers. The term was also used to define a specific location or rallying point for armies. *Standard* was the unification of terms meaning to "stand hard" in a specific area. This gave way to the use of the term to clarify the specific, shared meaning of a unit of measure. The king's standard for length allowed everyone in the kingdom to exchange goods based on a common understanding of weights and measures. This meaning evolved into the use of the term to clarify the value of something—the extent to which an object met specific standards, or expectations, for quality.

When we use the term *standards* in schools today, each of these uses continues to be relevant. Standards articulate the key points along a curricular pathway. Standards identify the points where we should gather to collaborate and communicate about what will come next. Standards for quality help articulate a shared language of the value of different levels of student work.

Standards as an Articulation of What Students Should Learn

In this chapter we are chiefly concerned with how standards are used to influence student learning. If standards articulate the desired outcomes for student learning, they must serve as the premise to guide teachers' and students' efforts in the classroom.

Since 1983, the primary concern of standards in U.S. education has been to define expectations for rigor that would stem the "rising tide of mediocrity" in our schools (National Commission on Excellence in Education, 1983, p. 5). Standards have been identified by various professional organizations, state departments of education, districts, and schools to clarify what students are to learn as a result of their learning experiences in school. Challenges in the implementation of standards have included issues with the standards themselves as well as their implementation in classrooms.

Concerns about the standards themselves include both the number of standards and their content. Concerns about the number are related to their feasibility and utility. One study determined that it would take about 21 years, rather than the typically allotted 13 years, to teach all of the standards identified by various content-based professional organizations at that time (Marzano, Kendall, & Gaddy, 1999). Concerns about content are typically related to the standards being deemed too specific or too ambiguous, or the extent to which they should emphasize factual knowledge versus conceptual understandings. Given these concerns, it is not surprising that the mantra underlying the recent development of the Common Core State Standards has been *fewer, clearer, and higher.*

Few national movements in the history of U.S. education evolved as quickly as states' nearly unanimous adoption of the Common Core State Standards. Through a process led by the National Governors Association and the Council of Chief State School Officers, the nation moved from a system of 50 different sets of state standards in mathematics and reading to a nearly uniform system of one set of mathematics standards and one set of reading standards. As noted, the mantra of the groups that established these standards—fewer, clearer, and higher—emerged from various concerns. Many people believed that the existing fragmented system created too many different targets for any sense of national direction to emerge. Additionally, there were concerns that many of the standards were articulated in a manner that was too broad to clarify the types of tasks that were evidence of proficiency and too convoluted to discern what students were supposed to do at specific grade levels. Finally, many felt a sense of urgency that the expectations for student performance embedded within the current systems of individual state standards and individual state assessments lacked the rigor necessary for students to be college and career ready in the 21st century.

As a field, education has been down this path before. *Ultimately, neither the standards themselves nor the new accountability tests designed to measure student progress toward those standards will do anything to improve student learning.* The leverage advantage of standards will only be realized if students—not only teachers—are empowered to use standards to guide their efforts. For this to occur, standards must be implemented in a manner that influences the curriculum, instruction, and assessment strategies that are used on a daily basis to intentionally connect students' efforts and productive conceptions of themselves as learners to those standards.

Transactional Utilization of Standards: Alignment Versus Adoption

There are two leverage errors associated with transactional implementation of standards, and they are described in the examples below. The first example demonstrates the challenges associated with the transactional alignment of standards. The second example articulates a more mindful process for implementing standards, but it may not result in a transformation of student learning.

Aligning Standards to Curriculum Documents as a Transactional Activity

A few months after the Common Core standards were widely adopted by states across the country, we heard of a number of school districts that had completed the alignment of their curricula to the Common Core. Curious, we engaged some of those districts in conversations about the process they'd used to do this important work. We were struck by the consistency of their responses. They'd gathered a group of curriculum leaders and laid out their curriculum maps. They looked at grids and check marks that had mapped their old standards and then looked at the new standards. They made new grids. They placed new check marks. The new document was proofed and edited. The new document was copied into new binders or uploaded to a curriculum management system.

It is critical to distinguish between merely recording whether current resources are *aligned to the potential* for addressing a standard, as opposed to intentionally developing curriculum, instruction, and assessments that are *explicitly designed to achieve* a standard. If the automobile makers in our earlier example had merely said that their current chemistry, physics, aerodynamics, and manufacturing processes were aligned with fuel efficiency (a dubious assertion, in any case), they never would have achieved such transformational results in such a short time.

Similarly, aligning any set of content standards to an existing curricular resource such as a textbook or to an existing published curriculum is a postmortem process. The curriculum has been established, the assessments have been developed, the textbook or other resources have been adopted, and, as an afterthought, someone records the alignment between the resources and the standards. The fact that a document results from this process and then sits in a binder or is uploaded to a web page has nothing to do with implementation. A set of science or mathematics standards could just as easily have been aligned to a cookbook—both discuss measurement, chemical interactions, following steps in a process, and so on. When standards are merely correlated or aligned to an existing curriculum, it is simply a transactional, clerical process that does not leverage the potential for standards to influence student learning. While the curriculum document has changed, the status quo of curriculum, instruction, and assessment will be maintained unless more explicit processes are utilized to leverage standards in a manner that connects them to classroom practice.

A more mindful approach to the alignment of curriculum to standards requires teachers to prioritize the standards to inform revised curriculum and instruction. Standards are specific; they describe critical components of what students are expected to know and do. For students to demonstrate proficiency in standards, they need specific, developmentally appropriate levels of challenge and support in the form of intentionally aligned resources, curriculum, instruction, and assessments.

Implementation Processes That Link Standards to Teaching

In his book *From Standards to Success*, Mark O'Shea (2005) describes how standards can be used to link classroom practice to student learning. He clarifies some of the core components of a standards-based classroom, such as the following:

- Standards are used to focus teaching.
- Standards are used daily as part of the classroom routine.
- Evidence of achievement of the standards is used to measure student progress.

O'Shea also clarifies the effectiveness of a variety of strategies and their utility in implementing standards, such as aligning district curriculum to standards, selecting textbooks that are aligned to standards, and establishing pacing guides linked to standards. The challenge of these approaches is that they articulate inputs for district office personnel or teachers but do not necessarily translate into a change in classroom practice. To guide teachers' use of standards in the classroom, O'Shea advocates the use of a five-step process:

- Step 1: Identify Standards… [teachers] identify the essential knowledge and skills to be included in their lessons.
- Step 2: Analyze Standards… [teachers] identify the statements in the standards and frameworks that describe what students are to know or be able to do.
- Step 3: Describe Student Performances… [teachers] write clear, explicit descriptions of products and behaviors that they expect from students.
- Step 4: Select Learning Activities… [teachers use] their knowledge of subject matter and students to anticipate student difficulties in learning and locate instructional resources.
- Step 5: Evaluate Students' Work… [teachers compare] student work samples with the descriptions of student performances in the lesson's objectives. (2005, pp. 32–35)

Through these steps, O'Shea provides a clear path for teachers, principals, and districts to consider when implementing—rather than merely aligning—standards to inform each teacher's practice. These steps clarify that the alignment of standards is not evidence of implementation of standards. Furthermore, these steps create a clear link between standards and each teacher's efforts to utilize effective instructional strategies in the classroom. However, the full potential of leveraging standards to improve learning will be best realized if the standards are used to strategically guide teaching and learning activities, processes, and goals in a manner that empowers students as the primary users of the standards.

Standards in the Context of the Five-Lever Framework: Linking Standards, Students, and Strategies

Standards have traditionally served two primary functions: to clarify what should be taught (content) and to articulate expectations for how work should be evaluated (quality). Both of these functions focus on the teacher as the sole user of standards. Through the lens of the Five-Lever Framework, standards are used to clarify what it is that students should learn (content) and to clarify where students and teachers should invest their efforts to ensure continued progress along a continuum of learning (quality). Specifically, we argue that standards are best leveraged when they create a direct, formative link between (1) students' ability to accurately self-assess their learning and (2) strategies students and teachers can utilize to focus their efforts to access next levels of learning.

Transformational change requires those implementing the change and those participating in the change to think differently about the nature of their work. If we are to empower students as the central users of standards, we need to better understand some of the assumptions that are made about student motivation, goals, and learning in different classroom environments.

Research on Performance-Oriented and Learning-Oriented Environments

In mid-November a middle school teacher attends a workshop on formative assessment and decides she will administer a pre-test to her science students at the start of the next unit to better discern where she should focus her efforts to address their learning needs. The day the new unit begins, she briefly explains the purpose of the assessment to her students and distributes copies to the class. Five minutes into the pre-assessment, she notices the frustration on her students' faces. One student starts crying. Another student folds the assessment in half and slams it on his desk. Finally, a student chimes in, "This isn't fair! Do you know what this is going to do to my grade point average?" The teacher pauses.

"I'm sorry, I didn't make it clear," the teacher replied. "This is just a pre-assessment. It won't count for a grade."

"Then why do we have to do this?" another student asked.

Would your students say the purpose of school is to learn? Or prove that they are smart? Perhaps the most significant impediment to using standards as a catalyst for transformation in curriculum, instruction, and assessment is related to perceptions about what students believe to be true about the purpose of schooling. Carol Dweck (2000, 2006, 2010) has spent much of her career researching what individuals believe about their capacity to learn and how different environments can support or extinguish their efforts to improve. In describing these environments, she distinguishes between environments that emphasize *performance goals* as compared to those that emphasize *learning goals* (Grant & Dweck, 2003).

Performance goals are pursued to demonstrate one's ability to accomplish a task. For example, if you already know how to do something and can gain token incentives by doing it again, there is much to gain by engaging in the task. By demonstrating competence you earn rewards or praise. However, if you don't know how to do something, an environment that emphasizes performance goals may punish you for trying. A hallmark of an environment that focuses exclusively on performance goals is that everything counts; there is no distinction between formative practice and summative evaluation. Learners may cope with the pressures of a performance environment by ignoring or avoiding tasks that they believe may reveal a lack of ability. This is unfortunate because individuals who attain expert status in their craft are tenacious about acknowledging and confronting areas of weakness until they improve (Ericsson, 2006). Or learners may cope by seeking short-cuts—such as cheating—to achieve the performance goal without engaging in the effort to acquire the intended learning. Not surprisingly, performance goal environments have been associated with negative patterns of learning (Deci & Ryan, 2000; Ryan, Gheen, & Midgley, 1998; Self-Brown & Mathews, 2003).

Conversely, learning environments value growth in knowledge and acquisition of new skills (Cherepinsky, 2011; Dweck & Elliott, 1983; Shepard, 2000). As Kaplan, Gheen, and Midgley (2002) report in their study on classroom goal environments and student behavior, classrooms with a strong learning goal environment "emphasize to students that their main purpose in being in school is to learn, improve, and master the material, rather than to demonstrate high ability and conform to the teacher's goals" (p. 204). In these environments, students are willing to engage in tasks that push them beyond their comfort zone. In fact, mistakes are valued as opportunities to clarify where to invest next efforts for improvement (Pedersen & Williams, 2004; Romanowski, 2004).

The anecdote at the beginning of this section illustrates the challenges that can occur when strategies that support learning goals are introduced into a performance goal environment. The teacher intended to use the assessment formatively to clarify the gap between current and desired levels of learning. The students, immersed in a performance goal environment, were solely focused on how the assessment would affect their grade. Similarly, norm-referenced grading systems of the past were well suited for classrooms that emphasized compliance in a transactional, performance goal environment. Standards-based systems that are focused on helping all students move toward or beyond clearly articulated criteria for quality can most effectively leverage standards by involving students in a system that empowers them to take ownership and monitor their own learning goals.

Different Answers to the Same Important Questions in Norm-Referenced Versus Criterion-Referenced Systems

Learners are driven by questions related to the relevance and rewards of the task and their perceptions of their ability to achieve success. The question "Why should I do this?" is related to students' interest in the utility of the task. The question "What does good look like?" is related to students' ability to regulate their effort to achieve desired results.

In an environment that emphasizes performance goals, grades often function as the sole currency of a token economy (Kohn, 1999). The answer to "Why should I do this?" is simply "Because it will be graded." Without this token incentive to engage in the performance goal task, it is assumed that students have no reason to engage in the task. In this context, teachers reward or withhold points and grades as a means to shape the behaviors of students (Ames, 1992). This premise lies at the core of a transactional system of learning because it assumes that students learn only when they are required to do work for points or grades. A number of studies argue that this assumption may be not only wrong but detrimental in the long term to student motivation and to student learning (Ames & Archer, 1988; Crooks, 1988; Dweck, 2000; Stiggins, 2001).

Traditionally, grading practices have been well aligned to norm-referenced systems (Guskey, 2011). In a norm-referenced system the standard for quality is a moving target depending on how other students perform. A few students earn the highest grade, a few students earn the lowest grade, and most students fall in the middle. In fact, *the central premise of a norm-referenced grading system is that only a few students will receive the highest grade*. The question "What does good look like?" cannot be answered in a norm-referenced system until after the evaluation has been completed. Given the ambiguity of what good looks like, students have little information as to how to invest efforts to improve. While few schools still grade on a norm-referenced curve, the residuals of norm-referenced grading remain: a system that is ambiguous in its criteria for quality but incredibly precise in its ability to quantify, rank, and sort students.

Unlike norm-referenced grading systems, a criterion-referenced, standards-based system requires grading practices that do not merely rank and sort students but create valid feedback loops to accelerate the progress of all students toward the articulated standard (O'Connor, 2002). *In a standards-based system, the premise is that all students can achieve the standard, given the opportunity to learn key concepts and skills associated with the standard.* The question "What does good look like?" is the premise for the system; standards are used to establish a shared understanding of quality, for teachers *and* learners to construct a clear picture of the learning they are working toward. The answer to "Why should I do this?" is to move your current level of performance to the next level. In a standards-based classroom with a strong learning environment, students know the goal, know where they are in relation to the goal, and have identified a clear path to close the gap between the two.

The differences between a norm-referenced system and a standards-based system are so powerful that they result in very different sets of behaviors. Consider two coaches preparing two different groups for a marathon.

The first coach has been selected to prepare a group of 30 people who have never run a marathon to *win* a marathon. In this norm-referenced system, there can be only one winner. The goal is to perform at a higher level than any other marathoner on the day of the race; the person who does so is the winner, and those who do not will be the losers. If the answer to the question "Why?" is "To win," and the answer to "What does good look like?" is "First place," it makes little sense to invest much time and energy in working with an athlete who will not place near the top of the pack. At the same time, it makes little sense for a slower athlete to bother training if it will afford her little chance of winning. The athlete's current level of skill will determine whether the coach invests time with the athlete and whether the athlete will invest much time in the coach. A few days into the training, many of the participants had already quit. By the day of the race, only a handful of the original group participated in the race.

The second coach has been charged with preparing a team of 30 people who have never run a marathon to *complete* a marathon. In this criterion-referenced system, the goal is to improve everyone's level of fitness to the point of being able to successfully cross the finish line. The answer to "Why?" is "To improve your level of fitness to accomplish something you never thought was possible." The answer to "What is good enough?" is "Finishing the marathon." Now the athlete's current level of fitness determines the strategy the coach and the athlete will use cooperatively to move each participant closer to the goal. The premise of this criterion-referenced system results in radically different levels of effort and strategy from the coach and the participants. On the day of the race, nearly all of the original group complete the task of finishing the race. All of the participants meet the goal of improving their level of fitness.

Notice in this example above that the task, or the assignment, was the same for both groups. However, the environments created by the two coaches resulted in dramatically different levels of investment to achieve the standard.

The Critical Distinction Between Activities and Goals

If we are to use standards to guide our efforts in a learning environment, then it is critically important that we clarify *what is being learned* as compared to the *activities that are being done* to engage in, and demonstrate progress toward, standards. In the framework in Robert Marzano's *The Art and Science of Teaching* (2007)—a framework that we discuss in further detail in our exploration of strategy in Chapter 4—the first question that teachers must consider when thinking about effective instruction is "What will I do to establish and communicate learning goals, track student progress, and celebrate success?" The premise of effective instruction is the teacher and student being clear about where they are headed. The first action step related to this establishment and communication of learning goals is to *distinguish between learning goals and learning activities*. This is a critically important step in the implementation of standards in the classroom because it raises important questions about whether standards will be utilized as a catalyst to inform progress toward learning or if tasks will be used as a means to accumulate points and grades. The example in the next section illustrates the critical distinction between tasks and goals and the importance of standards as a tool to help students invest effort in a manner that improves their learning.

Standards as Quality and Not Quantity

If students are to develop skills and understandings related to the standards, they need to have opportunities to practice the skills and understandings associated with those standards. Well-designed classwork and homework allow students opportunities to practice subskills, develop new understandings, try different strategies, and learn from mistakes as they approach (or move beyond) various standards for learning. Formative feedback about performances stated in terms of the standards can be used by teachers and students to clarify, and guide, where they should invest their efforts for producing work that is of high quality. Too often, students are aware of the *requirements or directions* of the tasks they've been asked to work on, but they don't connect those tasks to where they should *invest their efforts for improved learning as related to the standards.*

A Classroom Focused on Tasks

When students are told to do *pages 326–327, 1–23 odds,* teachers tend to get questions like *"How many points is each question worth?"* and *"Can we get extra credit?"* When students are told to *"Write a five-paragraph paper on topic X,"* teachers tend to get questions like *"Does it have to be exactly five paragraphs?"* and *"How short can the paragraphs be?"* When school is framed in terms of tasks, we tend to get questions about performance expectations associated with the structure of the task. This problem is likely to be compounded if the teacher in this classroom frames quality in terms of quantity: *list 3 main ideas, state 2 reasons, do 15 problems, and so forth.*

Two challenges are likely to occur in this classroom that may prevent students from making progress toward, and beyond, standards. First, in a classroom that focuses exclusively on tasks, students can come to see school as an endless loop of assignments, quizzes, and tests but don't understand—and eventually stop asking—how they are connected to anything meaningful. This is the Sisyphean approach to schooling; just when you get the boulder to the top of the hill, it rolls back to the bottom and the cycle of assignments, quizzes, and tests begins again. This loop results in what Denise Clark Pope describes as "doing school" (2001). The second challenge is that students may confuse arbitrary components of the task with essential characteristics of quality. Students may emerge from this classroom thinking that three ideas are better than one, five paragraphs are better than three, mathematical rigor and complexity are largely defined by the number of digits in the problems one solves, and the key to scientific inquiry is a lab report with a cover page that is printed in color.

In this classroom the teacher has unintentionally communicated a message that *what* students are doing is more important than *why* they are doing it and that *quantity* counts for more than *quality*. When asked the important "Why?" question, this teacher may be likely to respond with answers about points, grades, or *because it will be on the test*. Too often, rubrics contribute to this problem by communicating quantitative attributes of the task that are easy to measure rather than qualitative components of the learning goals that are important to measure (Brookhart, 2013).

The following example demonstrates how this approach can have a detrimental effect on the utilization of standards to transform student learning. Curricula can be written with the standards in mind, assignments can be developed with the standards in mind, yet unless students are empowered to assess their own work in relationship to the standards, those standards cannot be leveraged to improve student learning. In this example, 7th grade students were asked to write a personification essay (task) to demonstrate their understanding of, and inform others about, the scientific properties of an object (goal). The teachers logged in their curriculum guides that they were working toward standards related to "writing to inform," "using literary devices," and "expressing scientific ideas in writing." After the students completed their essays, the English teacher gave them a rubric (Figure 3.1) and asked them to assess their own work. Most students were able to easily do this and accurately assign a score to their own writing. The teacher then used the rubric to generate a standards-based grade.

With the rubric in mind, consider the following two writing samples from the assignment:

Writing Sample 1

Personification Paper

I am a little black rain cloud. I have a family of little black rain clouds. I have a boy rain cloud. He is seven. I have a girl rain cloud. She is four. We are all big. We are rain clouds.

I like to do things with my family. I like to rain on picnics. I like to rain on beaches. I like to rain on parties. I like to play baseball.

I like to play football. I like music. As you can see I like to do many things with my family.

I don't like to do things with my family. I don't like hockey. I don't like tennis. I don't like art. I don't like movies. I don't like pizza. As you can see, I don't like to do a lot of things.

As you can see, I am a little black rain cloud.

Score _____

Figure 3.1 | Poor Rubric for a Personification Paper

	Points		
	0	1	2
Title	No Title		Title
Details about family	1 or 0 details	2 or 3 details	4 or more details
Details about likes	1 or 0 details	2 or 3 details	4 or more details
Details about dislikes	1 or 0 details	2 or 3 details	4 or more details
Punctuation/ grammar	4 or more errors	2 or 3 errors	1 or 0 errors
Grade	9–10 pts. = Advanced; 7–8 pts. = Proficient; 4–6 pts. = Basic; 3–0 pts. = Minimal		

Writing Sample 2

Feeling Bi-Polar

For my entire life, I've been misunderstood. You see, contrary to the belief of people who envy me because of all of my pull, it's not easy being a magnet.

I'm seen by many as being demanding. I understand their concern; I am constantly trying to pull things my way.

"Can't you just leave me alone"? cries a paper clip that accidentally falls near my path.

"I have things to do myself", I reply. The frustration in my voice drips from between my prongs. "Who asked you to cling to my ankles anyway"?

"Connecting with others and holding on is in my nature", replied the paper clip. "I'm used to hanging around with my friends".

"I wouldn't know what that's like", the magnet sighed. "I don't have a family or friend of my own. Any time I find magnets that are similar to me, they find me to be quite repelling."

Score _____

When this example is shared with teachers, it is with a great deal of pain that they give 10 points and an "Advanced" to the rain cloud essay and 2 points and a "Minimal" to the magnet essay—yet those are accurate scores according to the rubric. The magnet essay is clearly a much higher-quality piece of writing. So what went wrong? The teachers planned the task with the standards in mind. The task was separate from, but aligned to, the goal. The teachers worked together collaboratively to plan the assignment. Students were even asked to self-assess.

The problem relates to our earlier statement about the two functions of standards: clarifying what students should learn (content) and articulating expectations for student performance across a continuum of learning (quality). As the essay example makes clear, standards must serve not only as the basis for planning activities, goals, and assessments; they must also be used to articulate the quality characteristics of a performance.

Common Leverage Errors Associated with Standards

The anecdote illustrates six problems, or leverage errors, that are indicative of the transactional implementation of standards:

1. *The process confuses what is easy to measure with what is important to measure.* Although it is easy to quantify numbers of ideas, numbers of paragraphs, and so on, these components have no relationship to the quality of student work.

2. *The process measures compliance with a task rather than the quality of the performance related to the learning goals.* It measures compliance rather than competence. Whereas it is relatively simple for a student to generate four ideas, it requires a lot of time, energy, and quality instruction to generate a compelling idea. A scoring guide emphasizes components of the specific task; a rubric emphasizes characteristics of quality.

3. *The rubric measures mistakes rather than misconceptions.* The second essay is considerably more complex than the first. The magnet essay has six mistakes in using end marks when writing dialogue, but the student author has only a single misconception about end marks.

4. *The rubric was used to measure, rather than guide, student work.* The introduction of this anecdote said that students were given the rubric for self-assessment after completing the essay. Although in this case the less time the students spend with this rubric the better, a well-designed rubric should be used throughout the instructional process. Generating a score for one's own work is not the same thing as self-assessing one's work. Quality self-assessment implies that learners are assessing the right things and using the self-assessment process to improve the quality of their work.

5. *The process uses a standards-based scale to communicate achievement, but the task does not generate evidence of progress toward a standard.* The use of descriptive terms (*Advanced* or *Minimal*), numbers (4 or 1), letters (*A* or *F*), or symbols (+ or –) has nothing to do with whether or not a system is standards based. A standards-based system measures clearly articulated standards for student progress using ongoing evidence of student work to discern each student's current level of progress. A standards-based system and terms typically used to describe proficiency are completely different things.

6. *The process may be correlated to standards, but it is not aligned to the standards.* The lesson may have been planned with broad standards in mind, but there is little evidence that standards have been used to create a clear, continuous thread among curriculum, instruction, and assessment.

A Classroom Focused on Learning Goals

A classroom focused on learning goals will use standards to help students clarify what they are working toward and how the assignments and activities will help them make progress toward those goals. Here, the teacher starts with the standards as the premise for the lesson and breaks the standard into smaller components, or learning goals, that can be shared with students. This approach starts with the teacher using *"What is it that I want students to learn, and how will I know that they've learned it?"* as the catalyst for planning lessons, activities, rubrics, and feedback that align content *and* quality.

Specifically, the English teacher chooses to focus on

Standard 3: Write narratives to develop real or imagined experiences or events using effective technique, relevant descriptive details, and well-structured event sequences.

b. Use narrative techniques, such as dialogue, pacing, and description to develop experiences, events, and/or characters.

d. Use precise words and phrases, relevant details, and sensory language to capture the action and convey experiences. (National Governors Association Center for Best Practices, 2009, p. 43)

First, the teacher breaks the standard into a few manageable learning goals and communicates those learning goals to the students so they understand where they should focus their efforts for quality. Students are given a self-assessment rubric to guide their work (Figure 3.2).

Second, the teacher focuses on targeted instructional opportunities and authentic learning tasks in his or her efforts to develop meaningful learning opportunities for students. Third, the teacher helps the student focus on quality aspects of the standards and learning goals rather than the components of the task. Finally, the teacher will use standards to help students determine which areas of focus are most worthy of their efforts by showing the students how to use the rubric to assess a few exemplary and nonexemplary writing samples. *Students will write narratives using relevant, descriptive details* begins to clarify *why* students are being asked to *write an expository essay*. Attaching these standards to an authentic task—*to write an engaging essay that personifies the scientific properties of an object*—clarifies how these skills will be used. Now, we are more likely to get questions related to the learning rather than the task: *What are relevant facts about my object? What is a specific detail? What is personification?* These questions can be used as pathways to guide teachers' and students' efforts to inform next steps in teaching and learning. *"Am I done?"* is replaced by more important formative questions such as *"Is it done well?"* and *"How can I make this even better?"*

Figure 3.2: Personification Essay Assignment Rubric

Learning Goal: Write a personification narrative using relevant descriptive details and well-structured event sequences.

Questions I Have	Characteristics of Quality	Evidence of My Understanding
	Uses dialogue, pacing, and description to develop characters.	
	Uses precise words, relevant details, and sensory language to convey experiences.	
	Accurately describes important scientific concepts.	

As I think about my work related to the learning goal above...

One thing I learned by doing this assignment is:

The part of this assignment I am most proud of is:

Balancing the Conversation Between Activities and Goals

Classrooms that empower students to accurately monitor their own learning produce remarkable results. Things teachers can do to help students focus on standards for learning include the following:

- Communicate learning goals that have been derived from the standards to students in student-friendly language.
- Help students clarify the learning goal from the task by having them write:
  Do [*task*] to develop your ability to [*learning goal*].
  in assignment notebooks and/or in homework headers.
- As much as possible, when providing tasks, rubrics, and feedback to students, try to use the language of the standards.

- Communicate learning goals that emphasize quality, not just quantity. (Do you want *5 ideas* or a *well-developed argument for or against a specific claim?*)

Leveraging Standards to Transform Assessment and Learning

To implement standards in a manner that transforms student learning, students need to be empowered to be the primary users of standards. To do this requires the use of strategies that directly connect the entire assessment process to students' learning goals and productive dispositions of themselves as learners to those standards. Strategies to involve students in the formative use of assessments *for* learning and prioritizing efforts to create a school culture that is committed to utilizing assessments *transformatively* are powerful means to make this happen and are described next.

Linking Standards to Student-Involved Classroom Assessment

Rather than focusing exclusively on how teachers will use standards to guide curriculum and instruction, Rick Stiggins (2002, 2004; Stiggins & Chappuis, 2005) focuses on how teachers can use standards to guide assessments that inform, rather than merely measure, students' learning.

In his work, Stiggins makes a key distinction between assessments *of* learning and assessments *for* learning. In the first case, assessments are used retrospectively to answer two questions: "What did the student learn?" and "What did the student fail to learn?" As Stiggins points out, these are the autopsies of the assessment world; the information that is derived is of little use to the individual who generated the data. The assessment is administered purely to make a judgment about the learner. These assessments stand in stark contrast to assessments *for* learning, which are guided by three very different questions: "Where am I now?" "Where am I going?" and "How do I get there from here?" Here, the learner is the central user of the assessment information.

In an article on how teachers can use student-involved classroom assessment to guide learning for all students and reduce achievement gaps, Stiggins and Jan Chappuis (2005) advocate for assessment systems that are mindful of four key conditions:

- Condition 1: Assessment development must always be driven by a clearly articulated purpose.
- Condition 2: Assessments must arise from and accurately reflect clearly specified and appropriate achievement expectations.
- Condition 3: Assessment methods used must be capable of accurately reflecting the intended targets and are used as teaching tools along the way to proficiency.
- Condition 4: Communication systems must deliver assessment results into the hands of their intended users in a timely, understandable, and helpful manner. (pp. 15–17)

In this framework, standards guide the educator's understanding of what is worthy to build each student's capacity to assess his or her own learning. If this is to be done in a valid way, the purpose, expectations, targets, and results must be derived from—and communicated in terms of—the standards.

Linking Standards to a System of Transformative Assessment

In his book *Transformative Assessment*, James Popham (2008) succinctly defines formative assessment as "a planned process in which teachers or students use assessment-based evidence to adjust what they're currently doing" (p. 6). Popham uses this definition as the basis for guiding teachers to consider how the implementation of four levels of formative assessment can raise achievement for all students. He defines these four levels as follows:

- Level 1 calls for teachers to use formative assessment to collect evidence by which they can adjust their current and future instructional activities.
- Level 2 deals with students' use of formative assessment evidence to adjust their own learning tactics.
- Level 3 represents a complete change in the culture of a classroom, shifting the overriding role of classroom assessment from the means to compare students with one another for grade assignments to the means to generate evidence from which teachers and students can, if warranted, adjust what they're doing.
- Level 4 consists of schoolwide adoption of one or more levels of formative assessment, chiefly through the use of professional development and teacher learning communities. (p. ix)

Here, Popham not only describes a pathway to change teaching, learning, and assessment but calls on educators and students to think differently about the norm-referenced, performance-oriented goal structures that permeate schools and classrooms and prevent the transformational use of assessments to guide students' and teachers' efforts. At the core of these levels of transformation are deeper, more thoughtful connections between students and teachers, teaching and learning, and standards and assessment.

Standards: A Recap

The hallmark of the *transactional* implementation of standards is that a flurry of activity occurs around structural, clerical tasks, but classroom practice, students' learning experiences, and student achievement remain largely unchanged.

The leverage advantage of standards is only realized when they are utilized in a formative manner to connect teacher's curricular, instructional, and assessment strategies to students' efforts and conceptions of themselves as learners. Rather than focusing on points, tasks, and one's standing relative to others, a standard-based system is largely concerned with developing a shared understanding of quality, generating accurate developmental feedback to inform one's efforts, and strategically utilizing effort to attain or surpass the articulated standard. To gain this advantage, students—not only teachers—need to be the primary users of standards.

Connecting Standards to the Chapter Vignettes

The vignettes at the start of this chapter illustrate how educators use standards in various ways. The first two demonstrate a transactional approach, and the second two show some of the more productive effects that can result from a transformational approach.

Reflections on Vignette 1: Alignment and Binders. This example is a classic case of a transactional process of correlating standards in an attempt to maintain the status quo. The assumption here is that the current curriculum, instruction, and assessment are adequate and implementation is merely a clerical task. Those involved have made no attempt to truly engage in a meaningful analysis of how the new standards are different from the old standards and the implications of those changes in terms of leveraging standards as a catalyst for developing aligned curriculum, instruction, and assessment. Moving this work to a website or a curriculum-mapping tool is also no more than a structural, transactional change in how the standards are used. Similarly, cutting and pasting 20 or 30 standards into each unit on a curriculum-writing template is evidence of a transactional approach to the clerical task of constructing a curriculum document that will result in classroom practice that merely perpetuates the status quo.

Reflections on Vignette 2: If a Few Are Good, More Must Be Better. Mr. Smith appears to hold high expectations for his students. However, from a standards-based perspective, he appears to have confused memorization with understanding and is focused on what is easy to quantify rather than what is important to assess—and what is important to assess is determined by the standards.

When Tony has teachers engage in the early stages of curriculum work, he asks them to mark the standards they currently teach. At this point in the process, teachers mark most—if not all—of the standards at their grade level or in their content area. Next, he asks them to mark the standards that have been formally assessed in the classroom. The number quickly dwindles down to less than a third of what was originally marked. Next, he asks teachers to mark the process or skill standards (for example, arguments and claims, mathematical reasoning) for which a common rubric aligned to that standard is used across more than one grade level. In many schools, teachers do not mark a single standard. Standards can be a powerful tool to leverage student learning, but only if they are used as a catalyst for a standards-based system that uses assessments formatively to inform each teacher's and student's efforts.

Reflections on Vignette 3: Prioritizing for a Purpose. A regional group of curriculum directors and teachers in the metropolitan Milwaukee area used this strategy to leverage standards when the Common Core State Standards were released. By collaborating across grades, schools, and districts, teachers engage in meaningful conversations about how the standards look to classroom teachers at various grade levels. The process of rank-ordering the standards requires educators to think critically about how they would prioritize the standards at their grade level. The explicit questions and discussions around assessment, assessment evidence, curricular sequences, and instructional strategies that support student progress from naïve to more sophisticated use of the content or skills articulated in the standards begin to build awareness about the purpose of the standards. The leverage advantage from focusing on standards occurs when those standards

- are positioned to offer meaningful and purposeful learning from the perspective of the learner;
- engage the learner in setting goals and selecting strategies to achieve them;
- inform the development of classroom assessments that give priority to what is most important in a discipline;
- are the premise for unit and lesson planning; and
- guide teachers' efforts to use responsive instructional strategies and provide concise, actionable feedback to students.

Reflections on Vignette 4: Standards Through Students' Eyes. In a standards-based system, students are the users and consumers of standards. This example demonstrates a strong culture of learning, the use of instructional strategies that support a standards-based system, and a system that clearly values and supports students' development of an accurate and positive conceptualization of themselves as active agents in the learning process. The student's ability to be meta-cognitive about her progress as a learner, to understand desired outcomes, and to monitor progress toward those outcomes bodes well for her progress in all areas.

Connecting Standards to the Global Prosperity Academy

The case that opened the introduction to this book describes several ways that the Global Prosperity Academy hoped to leverage standards to improve student learning. Although the staff implemented a standards-based report card, they did not implement a standards-based system to support the reporting tool. This omission can cause significant confusion among students and teachers.

For more than two decades we have watched new sets of standards come and go. Whether Goals 2000, No Child Left Behind, or myriad state-level curriculum goals adopted across the country, they have had little large-scale impact on student learning. The primary problem has not been that the standards are of poor quality, although in too many cases they have been so numerous that it is unrealistic to expect that teachers and students could legitimately address all of them in the course of semesters or school years.

Standards can give us clearer expectations for the level at which learning is expected to occur. Yet the goals and standards too often have not been supported by the instructional strategies and scaffolding necessary for students to reach them. Furthermore, learners too often have seen little relevance to their lives in the standards we have asked them to reach. They have little immediate reason to commit to achieving the standards other than extrinsic rewards and ill-defined consequences for falling short.

In our experience, the absence of major learning changes resulting from these standards has had less to do with the standards themselves and more to do with our collective inability to truly align standards to learning targets and learning experiences, and the absence of compelling, authentic reasons for learners to achieve them. Moreover, teachers have not been able to employ the robust, targeted, and leveraged instructional strategies necessary to move student learning as intended because they have been locked in a system that envisioned high levels of achievement for only a minority of learners.

Connecting Standards to the Kitchen Remodeling Analogy

Standards are clearly at play in the kitchen remodeling analogy; the challenge is the misalignment of the standards to the intended outcomes. As the remodeling project moved through various phases, an inspector surely came to ensure that the work being done was aligned to a set of standards associated with structural integrity, safe electrical wiring, and quality plumbing. These are *transactional* standards in that they exist to ensure the standards meet a minimal level of structural requirements associated with safety. However, the standards that guided the work weren't aligned to what the father and his child perceived to be the final assessment: the quality of the food. This misalignment between standards and assessment resulted in a leverage error; if the goal was to improve the quality of the food, other strategies could have been used to improve the capacity of the cook. This misalignment resulted in confusion and frustration after the project was completed.

Doing Less, Doing More

As with the other levers, using standards effectively most likely requires that we approach our work in a manner that differs from what we have

done in the past. Figure 3.3 summarizes the kinds of behaviors we should
do less of, and those we should do more of, if we want to use standards as
an effective lever for change.

Figure 3.3 | Leveraging Standards

Do Less of This	Do More of This
• Transactional alignment or correlation of new standards to status quo curriculum, instruction, and assessment	• Analyzing standards to consider the implications for changes in curriculum, instruction, and assessment
• Describing "what we cover" and "what we teach" in each classroom	• Analyzing how standards are assessed in a valid way and taught in a responsive way in each classroom; knowing that what is taught is less important than what has been learned
• Taking comfort knowing that teachers are aware of, and use, standards in their lesson planning	• Ensuring that students are aware of standards and use them to guide their efforts and assess their own work for attributes of quality
• Assuming that changing curriculum documents results in a change in the student learning experience	• Developing assessments and rubrics that are aligned to the content and ways of understanding articulated in the standards
• Assuming that the same articulated standards or grading scales result in similar expectations for quality work in each classroom	• Groups of teachers collaboratively analyzing and assessing common samples of student work to ensure a clear vision of, and a clear pathway to, quality work across grades and buildings
• Seeing teachers as the sole users of standards	• Developing systems that support teachers' and students' capacity to use standards to guide feedback and effort
• Treating all standards as being of equal importance	• Prioritizing standards to inform important decisions about resources to be allocated toward curriculum, instruction, and assessment

Reflecting on Standards: Questions to Ask on Monday Morning

- What is success in our school or district? How does our answer to this question align to the expectations we set? The data we collect and monitor?
- What is the amount or percentage of time I or others in my district spend talking about our shared expectations for quality as aligned to our expectations for success?
- When looking at agendas for board, faculty, team, and other meetings, to what extent do agenda items and meeting minutes deal with processes and criteria related to a shared vision for success? A shared vision of quality performance as kids progress through our school or district?
- Who are the users of standards in our school or district?
- Are students and teachers empowered as the users of standards to guide their efforts to influence student learning?
- Are standards and expectations for quality clearly articulated to stakeholders across our school or district in a manner that they all understand? Or do standards for quality work vary dramatically from teacher to teacher? Administrator to administrator?
- Are standards articulated across a continuum of learning in a manner that allows learners and parents to monitor and inform next steps in learning?
- To what extent is aligning current practices to new standards discussed as *the goal* of adopting new standards in our school or district? Or is the premise of new standards that if they are to be implemented effectively, they will require changes in curriculum, instruction, and assessment?
- To what extent do all students have the opportunity to learn and develop skills in the articulated standards?
- To what extent are individuals within our school or community comfortable with establishing lower sets of standards for some students and higher standards for other students? If so, how do these differences prevent some groups of students (consider race, gender, socioeconomic status, and other factors) from achieving high standards?
- To what extent do we find ourselves waiting to address new standards until teachers in previous grade levels have implemented and taught curricula aligned to those standards?
- To what extent are teachers waiting to address a student's learning needs, or absolving themselves from addressing a student's learning

needs, because the student's current level of skill is well below the articulated standard?

- To what extent do we expect that changing the standard will result in a better learning experience for students?
- How do we ensure that changing a standard is supported by an aligned, supportive change in curriculum, instruction, and assessment?
- What is the relationship between the cost of this change in standards—in terms of dollars, time, political chips, and other factors—and the expected results? Are there more direct, and more cost-effective, ways of addressing this issue?

Questions on Standards from the Students' Perspective

- How will the change in standards change each student's learning experience?
- How will the change in standards affect students' perceptions of themselves as learners? Do students see the standards as useful to guide their efforts to learn?
- Do the students understand that building competence in standards is the reason for the tasks they do in school?
- Can students answer these questions: Why are we doing this? What does a quality performance look like? What is my current level of performance? How can I close the gap between my current performance and the desired performance?
- Do students believe they have the capacity to achieve at high levels? Or do they believe some students are good in school and, therefore, smart—and others just aren't?
- How are students empowered to self-assess and direct their efforts in developing skills associated with the standards?
- How might students complete this prompt if the standards change is implemented effectively? *Before the change in standards, I used to _____, but now I _____.*

Look at the tables in Appendix D related to status quo, transactional, and transformational planning questions and examine the questions associated with standards. What types of questions do you typically hear in your school or district when you and your colleagues discuss standards? What types of questions do you typically ask?

Lever 4: Strategy

Vignette 1: New Textbooks and New Technology

After a two-year-long committee process and a contentious 4-to-3 school board vote, Ace Middle School purchases 1,500 new mathematics textbooks and 1,500 new touch-screen tablets with the goal of raising students' math achievement and creating 21st century learners. Two years into the initiative, achievement remains unchanged.

Vignette 2: New Evaluation Tools to Ensure Greater Accountability

Facing pressures to implement a new teacher evaluation process, an elementary principal does more than 200 classroom visits throughout the school year. He dutifully completes write-ups after each visit and sends notes to teachers expressing accolades and concerns. In May he spends countless hours writing final evaluation reports that articulate his rationale for each rating. On the last day of May he places an evaluation in each teacher's mailbox. That evening he starts getting e-mails; many teachers don't understand the rating process, and others think the ratings are unjustified. The principal wonders how he could have spent so much time giving teachers thoughtful advice throughout the year, yet their collective response is frustration.

Vignette 3: Collaborating on Student Achievement and Instructional Strategies

In early October a team of 8th grade teachers looks at classroom-generated data on student learning and acknowledges that students need to work on their ability to write effective arguments and claims. The teachers analyze their curriculum and realize that they teach only one lesson on this topic during the entire school year. They meet with the 7th and 6th grade teams and find that the specific language of arguments and claims is not taught in those grades. In an analysis of various rubrics used to score student writing in their middle school, they discover that the words *arguments* and *claims* don't appear on any of the rubrics. At a team meeting to work on curriculum related to this topic, they decide to develop a rubric element for arguments and claims for expository writing. About five minutes in, they realize that there is confusion about the semantics of *arguments* and *claims* in that different teachers are defining the terms differently, and they are struggling to come to consensus as to the specific characteristics of an *effective argument* and a *sound claim*. The team finally reaches consensus on each of the terms, as well as rubric descriptors articulating different levels of quality. The next week they bring in samples of student writing and agree on how to reliably apply the rubric to different levels of student work. One teacher describes a strategy she uses to teach students the distinction between an argument and a claim. Later that week the teacher visits a colleague's classroom and demonstrates the lesson while her colleague watches. The team members continue to share strategies, visit one another's classrooms, and score a few work samples together throughout the year. By the end of the year, all students can distinguish between an effective argument and a sound claim, and more than 95 percent of them can write a persuasive essay effectively using arguments and claims at the Proficient or Advanced level.

Definition, Misconception, and Opportunity

Definition: *Instructional strategies are the practices teachers use to help students deepen their understanding of content and improve their ability to use important skills.*

Strategy encompasses all of the components related to how educators use their knowledge of effective curriculum, instruction, and assessment to engage in practices that maximize student learning. Abundant research shows that effective teaching practices have a profound impact on student learning (Hattie, 2009; Haycock, 1998; Lemov, 2010; Marzano, 2007). Specific strategies such as effective use of formative assessment (Black & Wiliam, 1998), strategies that help students chunk content into manageable components (Miller, 1956), authentic reading and writing (Cunningham & Allington, 2010), and tending to student needs for emotional support (Hamre & Pianta, 2001) are just a few specific classroom practices that teachers can deploy to improve student learning. Even the words we use to present tasks to students or to affirm their effort can result in meaningful differences in student outcomes (Johnston, 2004).

Misconception: *Changing the structure, standard, or sample results in the deployment of more effective instructional strategies.*

Although changing the structure, standard, or sample can create an environment that is more conducive to the use of more effective instructional practices, those practices must actually be deployed in the classroom for students to have a more effective learning experience. For example, changing the school structure to allow for block scheduling will not be effective if 45-minute lectures are transformed into 90-minute lectures, any more than doubling the number of standards will double student achievement. Similarly, changes in standards should be closely connected to changes in instructional strategies that make achievement of the new standards a reasonable expectation. There is little reason to expect students to be able to achieve at higher levels without the support of more effective instructional practices.

Another misconception is that any research-based instructional strategy can be used at any time, with any student, and yield a significant effect on student learning. Knowing which strategy to use at which time (Marzano, 2007), and with what student or students (Voltz, Sims, & Nelson, 2010), is a critical part of the nuance and complexity of professional practice. The selection and application of instructional strategies must be done in a way that responds to the needs of the learners. Unless this match occurs, teaching is reduced to a transactional process—something that is done *to*, rather than *with*, students.

Opportunity: *Effective instructional strategies can be employed anywhere, at any time.*

Effective instructional strategies can be deployed at any time, in any classroom, by any teacher, with any group of students, provided that classroom teacher has focused opportunities to develop expertise in pedagogy, is open to feedback, and is in an environment that is committed to helping educators grow professionally (Marzano, Frontier, & Livingston, 2011). Each teacher's ability to use the right strategy, in the right way, at the right time holds the greatest potential to improve student learning.

A Comparison: Strategy in the Field of Medicine

The strategies professionals use have a profound impact on the results obtained by the individuals they serve. Before we discuss the role of strategy in education, let's consider an example from the world of medicine.

Suppose your 5-year-old daughter is not feeling well. Concerned, you bring her to the pediatrician's office to get a professional's opinion as to why she is ill and what might be done to help her get better. Once in the examination room, the physician looks at her tongue and tells you that her yellow and black bile are out of balance and she needs a good bleeding. He writes out a prescription for leeches and sends you on your way. Obviously, you'd be shocked at this response. The strategy he's articulated has not been considered to be best practice for hundreds of years. Amazed at the physician's diagnosis, you go back to the reception area and demand to see another doctor. The receptionist finds another physician, and after a few minutes you are in that physician's office.

The second doctor has your daughter sit on the examining table and go through a series of tests. She rattles off a series of numbers about your daughter's temperature, blood pressure, and other indicators and tells you that your daughter needs to spend more time working on being healthier. Frustrated, you ask to see a third doctor and head back to the waiting room.

Eventually, your daughter's name is called, and you and your daughter follow the nurse into yet another exam room. A few minutes later, the physician enters the room with a warm greeting, and while she washes her hands she starts an engaging conversation with your daughter. She has your daughter sit up on the examining table and asks her a series of questions about her school, her toys, and her symptoms. Meanwhile, she takes your daughter through the paces of a routine checkup. Next, the physician asks you a few questions about your daughter's medical history and her current symptoms. After a few more routine procedures and clarifying questions, the physician shares her diagnosis with you and talks about a prescription she recommends, a few simple treatments to do when the symptoms occur, and a few things to keep an eye on in the coming days. Your daughter, who normally doesn't like seeing the doctor, smiles as she leaves. On the way back to the waiting room your daughter says, "She's really nice."

Strategy at the Core of Professional Practice

As the medical example illustrates, physicians' knowledge of health and wellness and their ability to identify the gap between the current and the desired reality and to prescribe strategies to close the gap, as well as the strategies they use to engage each patient, make a profound difference for each patient's experience and outcomes. Different physicians utilize different strategies that can yield different results (Gawande, 2007). As a profession, teaching is no different. Our professional currency is understanding each learner's current level of understanding and the desired level of understanding, and using instructional strategies to close the gap between the current status and what might be. A teacher's ability to deploy strategies that are responsive to the needs of each learner has a strong effect on student learning. A classroom with an effective teacher is associated with growth in student learning at a rate that is three times greater than that in a classroom with a low-performing teacher (Barber & Mourshed, 2007).

Although differences in achievement across schools tend to grab headlines, achievement varies more from classroom to classroom than from school to school. In other words, there is "more variability in teacher quality within classrooms than across schools" (Stronge, 2010, p. 12). At the core of effective teaching is a reflective teacher who can use instructional strategies that are responsive to student learning needs.

Two relatively recent studies have synthesized an extremely broad range of research in the field of education. The first study, conducted by the National Research Council (Donovan & Bransford, 2005), utilized a comprehensive review of the literature to clarify what is known about how students learn. The second study, conducted by John Hattie (2009), used a quantitative meta-analytic process to identify specific strategies related to improving student achievement. While these studies used different methodological approaches, they reached remarkably similar conclusions about the nature of student learning and the implications for the use of instructional strategies to guide teachers' efforts to more effectively meet students' learning needs.

Three Principles Related to How Students Learn

Founded in 1863, the National Academy of Sciences has provided objective, research-based insight on matters of science, medicine, technology, and psychology to the federal government of the United States for 150 years. The academy uses teams of experts in their respective fields to gather, analyze, and synthesize research on dozens of topics, publishing the results through the National Research Council (NRC). In 2000 the NRC published a synthesis of research titled *How People Learn: Brain, Mind, Experience, and School* (Cocking & Bransford, 2000). The purpose of this book was to outline the broad principles of the relationship—and the disconnect—between what researchers have learned about how students learn and the structures and processes that are ubiquitously accepted as *school*. In 2005, the NRC published a second book on this topic, titled *How Students Learn: History, Mathematics, and Science in the Classroom*, to further describe and clarify how the concepts outlined in *How People Learn* could be applied to effective classroom practice. Central to both of these works are three well-established principles that support learning. The editors articulate these three principles as follows:

1. Students come to the classroom with preconceptions about how the world works. If their initial understanding is not engaged, they may fail to grasp the new concepts and information, or they may learn them for purposes of a test but revert to their preconceptions outside the classroom.
2. To develop competence in an area of inquiry, students must (a) have a deep foundation of factual knowledge, (b) understand facts and ideas in the context of a conceptual framework, and (c) organize knowledge in ways that facilitate retrieval and application.
3. A "metacognitive" approach to instruction can help students learn to take control of their own learning by defining learning goals and monitoring their progress in achieving them. (Donovan & Bransford, 2005, pp. 1–2).

Not only do the most effective teachers understand these principles; they embrace them and put them into operation through the intentional use of specific strategies that will honor learners' current understandings, integrate facts and concepts, and support learners' ability to be self-reflective as they strive to make meaning.

Using the Three Principles to Inform Instructional Practice and Leverage Strategy

These three principles can be utilized to guide decisions about the types of instructional strategies that can be leveraged to most effectively improve student learning.

Principle 1 clarifies that the individual doing the learning—not the curriculum or the teacher—is the central component of the learning process. Students are not empty vessels to be filled with knowledge. Students come to the classroom with a set of skills and understandings that are neither good nor bad; *they simply are*. What matters is how the learner is given the opportunity to build new knowledge from that existing knowledge. Principle 1 also makes a key distinction between knowing something for a test as compared to understanding something in a manner that allows learners to develop more accurate and more sophisticated ways of thinking than their initial conceptualization.

When teachers act on this principle, they use strategies that honor students' background knowledge. Specific strategies that might be utilized to these ends include the formative use of pre-assessments (Stiggins, 2002); capturing student interest and activating prior knowledge using mystery, controversy, personal experience, and *What if?* questions (Silver, Dewing, & Perini; 2012); taking time to activate schemas and make meaningful connections (Keene & Zimmerman, 2007); and identifying errors in thinking (Marzano, 2007).

Principle 2 clarifies the balance between factual knowledge and conceptual frameworks and articulates how those two components can be mutually supportive. Education is often mired in arguments about factual knowledge versus conceptual frameworks (phonics versus whole language, computation versus mathematical reasoning, important dates versus historical thinking). The reason these either-or debates are so difficult and contentious is that they're often framed as a false dichotomy. Factual knowledge is meaningless unless it can be organized and put into operation through broader conceptual frameworks. Conceptual frameworks are useless unless they can be put into operation using specific facts.

Teachers who act on this principle utilize instructional strategies that help students integrate factual knowledge *and* conceptual frameworks. For example, Jay McTighe and Grant Wiggins (2013) describe specific strategies that can be used to help students develop understanding as aligned to different types of learning goals. Direct instruction that uses strategies such as lecture, advance organizers, and guided practice can be effective when the goal is to help students acquire factual knowledge. Facilitative teaching that uses strategies such as problem-based learning and reciprocal teaching can be effective when the goal is to help students construct the meaning of key concepts. Teaching for transfer of learning to new and novel situations requires teachers to utilize strategies that help students draw inferences and make connections among facts *and* concepts.

Principle 3 clarifies the role of the learner as *the* active agent in the learning process. Ultimately, learning is not conducted through an external act by a teacher but, rather, occurs through an internal set of processes governed by the learner. Learning is a process of thinking about one's own thinking. To recognize this principle is to understand that the most profound questions that further learning are rarely asked on a test; they come from the learner. Metacognitive questions such as "What does this mean?" "Why doesn't this make sense?" and "Why does this happen?" are the most important questions asked of any learner. According to this principle, the most critical role a teacher can play is to empower students to honor these questions to guide their learning. Too often, learners see questions as evidence of ignorance rather than as pathways to understanding. If students are to reach their full potential, teachers need to create classroom environments where it is OK for students to acknowledge that they are confused, that they are struggling with challenging new ideas and skills, and that they don't understand yet (Dweck, 2006).

When teachers act on this principle, they strive to involve students as *the* active, reflective agent in the assessment process (Stiggins, 2006). For example, teachers may use strategies such as think-alouds (Keene & Zimmerman, 2007) while reading a story, solving a math problem, or analyzing a historical document to model for students the ongoing internal dialogue that adults utilize when trying to make sense of something. Students may be taught to articulate their own learning goals, reflect on those goals, and monitor their own progress (Marzano, 2007). Rather than teachers being the primary users of rubrics to grade student work, a classroom that honors the importance of meta-cognition may teach students to use rubrics to accurately assess their own work and engage in formal reflective processes such as peer conferences (Carr & Harris, 2001).

A classroom that honors the principles outlined in *How Students Learn* (Donovan & Bransford, 2005) would look more like an artisan colony than an assembly line. Students would likely be engaged in tasks that afforded multiple pathways into the content being taught and opportunities to present their understanding in different ways. The ambiguity of navigating the connections between content knowledge and conceptual frameworks would result in students and teachers asking questions of each other—questions without easy answers. The time and space given to students to be reflective about their own learning would mean students were engaged in a lot of *thinking*—reflective writing and discourse that could not be assessed by another as right or wrong but could only be valued as useful or distracting in relation to each learner's circuitous pathway between naïve and sophisticated understanding.

These three principles clarify what learning is *not*. Learning is not a passive process where one is merely asked to sit quietly and receive knowledge. Learning is not simply the accumulation of additional knowledge or facts recorded through a series of assignments that requires students to *fill in the blank*. Learning is not coverage of content and the assignment of grades. As Grant Wiggins and Jay McTighe (2005) point out, classrooms that ignore these principles tend to plow through content or keep kids busy with activities that aren't aligned to meaningful outcomes. Neither of these approaches yields much understanding.

Using Meta-analysis to Transcend the Limits of Any One Study

Meta-analysis attempts to bring a broader, more balanced view of educational research to guide practitioners' efforts to leverage professional practice that results in student learning. Rather than focusing on any one study to inform practice, meta-analysis acknowledges that different studies will produce varied results due to the complexities of the act of teaching (as related to the skill and experience of the teacher using the strategies, the fidelity of the use of various strategies, the students in the sample, and other factors), variability among students (in age, interests, skills, background, preferred modalities for learning, and other factors), and the reliability and validity of the research design itself. By looking across the results of dozens of studies on the same topic, meta-analysis can determine a general effect associated with different strategies. This result is reported in terms of an *effect size*. An effect size of 1.0 (about 115 points on the SAT and 5 points on the ACT) would mean that students who had access to the strategy scored an average of one full standard deviation higher than students who did not have access to that strategy.

Several years after the publication of *How Students Learn*, another study was published that made a series of recommendations for effective practice based on a synthesis of research in the field. The study, *Visible Learning: A Synthesis of over 800 Meta-analyses Relating to Achievement* (Hattie, 2009), along with its follow-up further describing implications for classroom practice, *Visible Learning for Teachers: Maximizing Impact on Learning* (Hattie, 2011), was conducted and written by John Hattie of the University of Auckland. The most comprehensive study ever conducted in the field, it drew from meta-analyses that included nearly 53,000 studies and a sample of about 240 million students.

Hattie synthesized and rank-ordered a series of more than 100 different influences on student achievement. He then categorized those influences as being associated with the student, home, school, teacher, curricula, or teaching practices. Contrary to conventional wisdom, Hattie found that influences associated with the home and the school have a less significant effect on student learning than the characteristics of the teacher, the quality of the curricula, and the quality of the teaching.

In looking at specific practices across all of those influences, Hattie found that instructional strategies associated with the quality of teaching such as the use of Response to Intervention strategies and providing targeted feedback were among those with the highest effect sizes in influencing student learning—1.07 and .75, respectively. Conversely, school-level practices associated with structure and sampling such as changing school calendars, multi-age classrooms, and grade retention were among those with the smallest, and even negative, influences on students learning—their effect sizes were .09, .04, and −.13, respectively.

Across all of the practices synthesized through Hattie's research, he found that the average effect of any practice is about .40 standard deviations. In other words, few practices actually have a negative effect on student learning, which means even the least powerful practices have a marginal effect on student learning. Hattie calls the effect size of .40 the "hinge-point" because it is the point at which the effect on student learning is likely to be better than average in making a "visible difference to student learning" (2011, p. 14).

The hinge point requires us to think differently about the criterion we establish for effectiveness. *"Did this strategy improve student learning?"* is not the most important question to ask when analyzing current practice or considering the value of a change in practice. *"Did this strategy improve student learning at a level beyond those effects associated with any random strategy?"* is a far more telling question related to the effectiveness of our efforts. Is the time, effort, and energy of a new structural approach to scheduling or a new sampling approach to ability grouping worth the effort if it is associated with only a miniscule improvement in student learning? If the goal is to improve learning for students, might it make more sense to leverage classroom instructional strategies that are associated with effect sizes that are 10 to 15 times greater? The concept of the hinge point is critically important to frame conversations about what works in schools. It is the starting point for focusing discussion and consideration of practices that might not just leverage student learning but *most effectively and efficiently leverage student learning.*

How Hattie's Meta-analysis Validates the Five-Lever Framework

Another key takeaway from Hattie's work is that the teacher, teaching practices, and curricula all have an effect size that is beyond the .40 hinge point. Of the 138 practices rank-ordered for their level of effectiveness by Hattie, 26 of the top 30 effect sizes (ranging from .57 to 1.44 standard deviations) are related to teaching, the teacher, and curricula (2009). In other words, focusing on building teachers' capacity to deploy research-based instructional strategies—such as formative assessment, meta-cognitive strategies, teaching specific problem-solving techniques—may inoculate leaders from committing leveraging errors. Conversely, structure and sampling practices—such as open versus traditional classroom spaces, multigrade classes, class size, and ability grouping—which we've identified as frequently being subject to high-effort, low-yield leveraging errors, were found by Hattie to have the smallest effects on student learning. The components associated with instructional strategies and conceptions of self were found to be, on average, eight times more effective at improving student learning than those practices associated with structure and sampling (Hattie, 2009, p. 244).

This is *not* to say that the components associated with structure and sample are irrelevant. We are arguing that structure and sample create a context—but are not necessarily a critical attribute—where standards, conceptualization of self, and instructional strategies can be more effectively leveraged to influence student learning.

What is most impressive about *Visible Learning* is the scope of the analysis Hattie utilizes to discern *what is known* in the field. What we find to be most remarkable about *Visible Learning* is the conclusion Hattie reaches to discern *what matters* in the field. From millions of students, thousands of studies, and hundreds of components that influence student learning, he concludes his work by arguing that learning occurs most effectively when two things happen: (1) each teacher sees his or her classroom through the eyes of his or her students, and (2) each student sees him- or herself as his or her own best teacher (Hattie, 2009, p. 238). Through this lens, it is relatively simple to prioritize the strategies that are associated with the highest levels of student learning.

For teachers to *see through the eyes of the student* means the most effective strategies will create a direct link between teachers' standards for quality and students' conceptions of themselves as learners. Students don't wake up thinking about lesson plans. Students rarely walk the hallways awed by the elegance of the distributive property or sit down in classrooms thinking about the distinction between good writing and great writing. The most effective teachers do not point to these realities as a liability within each student. The most effective teachers embrace this fact as a starting point for utilizing strategies that engage students, actively monitoring student learning and then adjusting their use of a variety of instructional strategies to guide students along a continuum from apathy to understanding. As James Popham (2008) points out, "We find too many teachers paying attention to the instructional procedures they use, rather than to what happens to their students as a result of those procedures" (p. 53). Hattie further clarifies how the most effective teachers respond to their students by stating:

When teachers see learning occurring or not occurring, they intervene in calculated and meaningful ways to alter the direction of learning to attain various shared, specific, and challenging goals. In particular, they provide students with multiple opportunities and alternatives for developing learning strategies based on the surface and deep levels of learning some content or domain. (Hattie, 2011, p. 15)

With this quote, Hattie not only articulates the importance of teachers being responsive to student learning needs, *but also clarifies the intent of their utilization of instructional strategies is to empower students with their own learning strategies.* This connects seeing through the eyes of students to helping students see themselves as their own best teacher.

To help all students *see themselves as their own best teacher* means the most effective teachers will use strategies that create a direct link among standards, curriculum, instruction, assessment, and the effort students put forward to guide their own efforts to improve. Through this lens, standards, learning goals, rubrics, formative assessments, and goal setting are the tools that students are taught to use to guide their path from engagement to autonomy. As we discussed in the previous chapter, a rubric is no longer a transactional component to be used at the end of a sequence of learning to justify a grade. A rubric is now a transformational tool used to guide the curriculum, to create a shared understanding of how developmental feedback can be used to make progress, and to develop each student's language of self-assessment. The language of quality articulated in a rubric will have the greatest leverage when it is used to guide teachers' and students' collective understanding of what quality looks like, develop students' current understanding of their work as related to the standards for quality that have been established, and guide the strategies students will use to move from the learners they are now to the learners they haven't become quite yet.

There is remarkable consistency in the broad findings of *How Students Learn* and *Visible Learning.* Addressing student preconceptions and helping students integrate factual knowledge *and* conceptual frameworks are clearly aligned to the importance of teachers seeing their classrooms through the eyes of their students. Using a meta-cognitive approach to teaching is clearly aligned with helping students see themselves as their own best teacher. Given the broad consensus for what works in the field, why is it so difficult to leverage more effective instructional strategies in every classroom to further improve student learning?

Obstacles to Leveraging Instructional Strategies

A challenge in any profession is determining which specific practices are most likely to produce desired results. Although it seems there should be a set of "best practices" or tacit knowledge that all practitioners develop simply by participating in the field, the reality is more complex. We have seen two primary challenges that impede educators' collective ability to more effectively leverage classroom strategies in a manner that maximizes student learning needs. These two factors are related to the use of research to inform practice and the predictable, but complex, nature of developing expertise. At the intersection of these two challenges is the leveraging error most typically associated with the implementation of instructional strategies: transactional expectation of strategies as a proxy for thoughtful implementation.

Misusing a Good Thing: Transactional Implementation of Research-Based Strategies

Simply identifying, communicating, and then expecting the use of more effective instructional strategies is not enough to influence teacher expertise or improve student learning. This transactional expectation of improved use of strategies fails to honor the complexity of teaching. The leverage advantage of instructional strategies is most powerful when educators are able to utilize strategies in a manner that honors the research base from which those strategies were derived and that is flexible enough to be responsive to the needs of students. Effective utilization of a new strategy in any field takes time and requires practitioners to move along a circuitous path from initial, novice attempts to expert use. Unfortunately, strategies are too often presented as a set of transactional tasks to merely be marked on a checklist. Two examples of how some educators have committed the leveraging error in their implementation of research-based strategies are the misuse of the Seven-Step Model for Lesson Planning developed by Madeline Hunter, and the misuse of the book *Classroom Instruction That Works* by Robert Marzano, Deborah Pickering, and Jane Pollock (2001).

Hunter's Seven-Step Model

In 1976, UCLA professor Madeline Hunter and her colleague Doug Russell wrote a book chapter titled "Planning for Effective Instruction: Lesson Design." Their intent was to identify and describe the components that they had noticed were present in many of the effective lessons they observed: anticipatory set, objective or purpose, instructional input, modeling, checking for understanding, guided practice, and independent practice. Soon these components were incorporated into what became widely known as "Hunter's Seven-Step Model," and by the mid-1980s they had become a cornerstone of many teacher evaluation programs (Fehr, 2001). In many schools, teachers were expected to describe their lessons in terms of Hunter's model, and supervisors determined the fidelity of the lesson based on alignment to the model. The model became so ingrained (and prescribed) as a framework for required lesson plans and as the basis for classroom observations that by the mid-1980s, teachers were complaining about being *Hunterized* (Simmons, 2004). Their complaints were warranted.

Even Hunter realized that her model was being used as a checklist for compliance rather than as a framework to inform professional practice. In her article "What's Wrong with Madeline Hunter?" (1985), she sought to clarify the intent of the seven steps and described eight problems she'd noted in the implementation of her work:

1. The misunderstanding that every element must be used in every lesson.
2. If a little is good, more must be better (e.g., using four anticipatory sets in a single lesson).
3. Observers judge [lessons] without understanding teachers' rationale for their decisions.
4. Too much is expected of teachers too soon; the framework is simple in conceptualization but complex in practice.
5. Teachers were being taught how to use the model, but administrators were not.
6. One-shot exposure to the framework, and then moving on to the next initiative.
7. Once trained, administrators and teachers think they are finished learning about the model.

8. Leaders are not adequately trained to implement and support teachers' development in learning the model. (pp. 59–60)

These problems resulted in frustration among teachers and a failure to reap the potential benefits of the framework. Despite Hunter's concerns, transactional deployment of her framework persisted. Two years later, Patricia Wolfe (1987) attempted to further clarify the intent of the model on behalf of Hunter. In her article "What the 'Seven Steps Lesson Plan' Isn't!" Wolfe clarified that Hunter's framework was not intended to be used as a rigid set of steps to be followed but, rather, as *a set of elements to consider when engaged in planning.* As Wolfe clarified, "The 'dissidents' are right! Those seven instructional elements are not a recipe to be followed step by step in every lesson; they are elements to be considered when planning instruction" (p. 70).

At the core of Hunter's and Wolfe's concern was the disconnect between teachers using the model to clarify and guide the strategies used to plan lessons that would most likely improve student learning, and the implementation of the model as a transactional, rigid framework to be followed for every lesson for purposes of evaluation. As Hunter stated, "Models are judged on their ability to guide behavior, predict outcomes, and stimulate research, not on their being the final answer" (1985, p. 60).

It would be satisfying to say that by the late 1980s we'd learned our collective lesson from the misapplication of Hunter's work. Unfortunately, 20 years later, another model designed to guide teachers' efforts toward more effective utilization of instructional strategies was also subject to the limitations of the leveraging error of transactional expectation.

Classroom Instruction That Works

In their seminal book *Classroom Instruction That Works* (2001), Robert Marzano, Deborah Pickering, and Jane Pollock used meta-analysis to identify the following nine instructional strategies associated with particularly strong effects on student learning:

1. Identifying similarities and differences
2. Summarizing and note taking
3. Reinforcing effort and providing recognition
4. Homework and practice

5. Representing knowledge
6. Learning groups
7. Setting objectives and providing feedback
8. Generating and testing hypotheses
9. Cues, questions, and advance organizers

The opening chapter of the book described in detail the opportunities and limits of meta-analysis, as well as the broad range of unknowns around the implementation of various strategies. These unknowns included questions about the effectiveness of various strategies in specific subjects, at specific grade levels, and with specific students. For each strategy the authors articulated the supporting research base and underlying theory, thoughtfully described specific classroom practices associated with each of the strategies, provided real-world classroom examples, and shared specific tools and templates that teachers and students could utilize to scaffold and guide student thinking. The final chapter described the need to be sensitive to the use of different strategies at different points in the teaching process. For example, some strategies are better suited to the beginning of a unit, whereas others are more suitable at the end. In 2003, the book was followed by *Classroom Management That Works* (Marzano, Marzano, & Pickering, 2003) to articulate a research-based synthesis of the most effective classroom management strategies.

Using these books as a guide, districts across the United States started to engage in important and meaningful efforts to focus on how teachers could best use these strategies in classrooms to maximize student learning. This focus allowed schools to prioritize professional development on the use of specific, potentially powerful strategies and the nuances associated with effective deployment. However, some schools and districts used a more didactic, transactional approach. As Hunter had experienced more than 20 years earlier, Marzano also saw his work subject to the rigid implementation of a model as a checklist recipe of transactional expectation for prescribed practice rather than as a framework *intended to guide and potentially transform* professional practice. In his article in *Phi Delta Kappan* titled "Setting the Record Straight on 'High-Yield' Strategies" (2009), Marzano noted three specific concerns in the application of his *What Works* titles:

1. Focusing on a narrow range of strategies, such as using the nine instructional strategies identified in *Classroom Instruction That Works* as the sole basis for evaluation.

2. Assuming "high-yield" strategies must be used in every class, despite the fact that "a specific instructional strategy is effective only when it is used in the specific situation for which it was designed" (p. 34).

3. Assuming that high-yield strategies will always work. Research in the social sciences typically describes an average effect, depending on how well the strategy is used, when it is used, and other factors. This means sometimes the strategy will have a positive effect, sometimes it will have no effect, and sometimes it may actually have a negative effect. The question at hand is which strategies tend to have a greater effect if used the right way, at the right time.

As we observed in our explanation of the misapplication of Hunter's work, Marzano makes a number of points that are critically important for teachers and administrators to avoid the leveraging error of transactional expectations of more effective instructional strategies. Teaching is a complex process. Marzano is *not* saying that we don't know what works; he is saying that professionals must bring a sense of nuance and responsiveness to the frameworks they use to inform professional practice; there is both an art and a science to utilizing instructional strategies in a manner that is most responsive to student learning needs.

To clarify and place the findings of the *What Works* books into the context of a comprehensive framework honoring the complexity of the utilization of instructional strategies, Marzano wrote *The Art and Science of Teaching* (2007). Here, he describes instructional strategies in the context of a comprehensive model for effective classroom practice. In this model, the pathway to effective practice is guided by considering the interrelationships among 10 instructional design questions and their accompanying research-based strategies and behaviors:

1. What will I do to establish and communicate learning goals, track student progress, and celebrate success?

2. What will I do to help students effectively interact with new knowledge?

3. What will I do to help students practice and deepen their understanding of new knowledge?

4. What will I do to help students generate and test hypotheses about new knowledge?

5. What will I do to engage students?

6. What will I do to establish or maintain classroom rules and procedures?

7. What will I do to recognize and acknowledge adherence and lack of adherence to classroom rules and procedures?

8. What will I do to establish and maintain effective relationships with students?

9. What will I do to communicate high expectations for all students?

10. What will I do to develop effective lessons organized into a cohesive unit?

As teachers consider these questions and the specific research-based strategies and behaviors that support them, it is important to remember that all questions need not be considered equally at all times. The questions are divided among those that need to be addressed by the teacher as routine behaviors in every lesson (Questions 1 and 6), those that need to be addressed when considering how to teach academic content (Questions 2, 3, and 4), and those that need to be enacted on the spot (Questions 5, 7, 8, and 9). The art and science of teaching involves applying the research-based strategies that support each of the questions into meaningful, coherent lessons for students across each class period as well as across each unit of study (Question 10). The model is not a checklist that must be deployed every class period but, rather, a framework to keep in mind as teachers plan and implement strategies across a lesson, monitor student progress, and modify instruction to ensure student needs are effectively met.

The Net Effect

When mindful implementation of instructional strategies is reduced to checklists of expected behaviors, teachers and administrators become frustrated. Administrators find themselves generating long paper trails for summative evaluations that do not improve teachers' practice. Teachers find themselves frustrated by expectations that seem so specific that they are unrealistic. Teachers close their doors and teach using their preferred approach. Administrators move on to the next initiative. The underlying premise is "As long as no one complains, we'll quietly coexist." This stalemate prevents the entire field from making meaningful improvements.

The Nature of Expertise

Expertise is the ability to use specific skills in a complex field to attain desired results (Ericsson, 2006). Developing expertise in a single surgical technique can take years. Developing expertise in a complex game like chess or in a complex task like playing the violin takes focused, specific practice across hours, days, and years. Teaching is a complex field. On any given day, teachers are required to make thousands of decisions related to organization, management, and execution of specific strategies that are most conducive to each student's learning needs, the needs of the entire classroom, and the expectations and requirements of the school, the district, the community, the state, and the nation. No two students are the same. No two days are the same. Developing expertise in teaching is remarkably similar to developing expertise in other complex fields.

The characteristics of the pathway taken by individuals who develop expertise are well documented in research studies across a variety of domains (Ericsson, Krampe, & Tesch-Romer, 1993; Simon & Chase, 1973). Understanding the research on expertise and expert performance involves two critical concepts. First, expertise is a function of hard work and not innate talent. Although variations in human performance will always be present, any individual can remarkably improve the skills associated with any chosen domain. Second, it is not time alone that results in expert performance but, rather, how an individual uses that time to engage in deliberate practice developing specific skills in that domain.

The deployment of any complex skill requires a significant amount of time and practice. A group of teachers may use a new strategy and express concerns that the approach is ineffective because after initial attempts, students didn't learn as well as when the previous strategy was used. However, when developing proficiency in a new skill or strategy, even experts are prone to errors (Ericsson et al., 1993). Perseverance through this implementation dip is essential if new levels of effectiveness are going to be reached. Principals and supervisors may unintentionally prevent teachers from persevering through this learning curve by unwittingly creating a culture where efforts to grow and improve are seen as liabilities. Because of the challenges associated with persevering through the inevitable implementation dip, we never see the full capacity of the new instructional practice come to fruition. In an era of high-stakes teacher evaluation, we fear that the fuel that powers expertise—acknowledging the need to grow, watching other practitioners, strategically embracing trial and error, and engaging in deliberate practice—may be seen by many teachers as too hazardous to touch. Harnessing the leverage advantage of instructional strategies requires us to use research-based instructional practices in a manner that honors the limits and lessons of educational research while ensuring thoughtful implementation of new strategies. What generalizations can we make from the research on expertise? First, experts break their craft into smaller, manageable pieces to facilitate deliberate practice. A golfer on the path toward expertise may focus on the specific nuances of short uphill putts that break to the left. A teacher on the path toward expertise may focus on strategies that support and scaffold the complexity and accuracy of disengaged students' responses to open-ended questions.

Second, schools and districts must acknowledge that acquiring expertise in teaching requires the development of a complex, challenging, and demanding set of skills—and the acquisition process is lengthy. Expertise is not acquired upon completion of a certification program or with the granting of tenure. As with any complex set of skills—whether becoming a concert violinist, a skilled surgeon, or an outstanding teacher—expertise is acquired through years of deliberate practice, and mastering all of the strategies associated with effectiveness can occupy an entire career.

When schools and districts inadvertently associate the granting of tenure with the demonstration of expertise, they send a message to teachers that they have finished growing; their practice has reached the apex. Unfortunately, this mind-set is anchored in the semantics of many school, district, and state department of education frameworks for evaluation. Teachers who are struggling are categorized as being "in need of improvement." When a tenured teacher is struggling in the classroom, the strongest disciplinary measure an administrator can take short of dismissal is to put the teacher on *an improvement plan.* Consider those semantics. What type of system is in place when only those who are failing are "punished" through a plan of improvement? If expertise is acquired through deliberate practice over many years, who *shouldn't* be on an improvement plan?

As a profession, our conceptual understanding of expertise needs to shift from a model in which expertise is largely assumed to one in which expertise is derived from a career of intentional, deliberate practice. Effective use of new instructional strategies may require time to observe the strategy being used by an experienced practitioner; the opportunity to try the strategy and receive and act on focused, nonjudgmental feedback; and the opportunity to engage in deliberate practice to learn how to use that particular strategy (Marzano et al., 2011).

Transformational Systems That Support Teacher Expertise

Transactional implementation of models that prescribe a few instructional strategies as the goal of effective teaching are of particular concern during this era of high-stakes teacher evaluation. In a recent *Educational Leadership* article, Mielke and Frontier (2012) argue that as we roll out new teacher evaluation models, we're in danger of ignoring the lessons we learned while rolling out other high-stakes assessments:

> Like high-stakes student assessment, high-stakes teacher evaluation threatens to be an occasional event that is disconnected from day-to-day teaching and learning, producing results that do not help teachers improve their performance and placing teachers in a passive role as recipients of external judgment. (p. 10)

If we are to avoid this outcome, we need to empower teachers as ongoing users of information about their instructional practice in a manner that informs their efforts to become expert.

In the book *Effective Supervision: Supporting the Art and Science of Teaching*, Marzano and his colleagues (2011) argue that any effective system of supervision—that is, one that results in the development of teacher expertise that will lead to improved student learning—must have the following five components:

1. **A well-articulated knowledge base for teaching,** including shared understanding and language describing specific strategies and behaviors found in effective practice

2. **Opportunities for focused feedback and practice,** with feedback coming from sources including students, colleagues, or self-assessment via video recording

3. **Opportunities to observe and discuss expertise** in various components of effective practice, with observations via classroom visits or video observation

4. **Clear criteria and a plan for success,** including shared understanding of various levels of quality for effective practice and the ability to self-assess and close the gap between current and desired practice

5. **Recognition of expertise** via a system that uses clear descriptors and high standards of quality

These components require teachers and administrators to think differently about the nature and nurture of good teaching, what it means to be a professional, and how to go about the process of improving each teacher's expertise in utilizing instructional strategies that improve student learning. We've found a number of high-leverage administrative strategies that support the five components listed above and can be utilized to support teachers' development of expert utilization of classroom strategies:

- Use frameworks for effective practice (Danielson, 2007; Marzano et al., 2011; Strong, 2011) as the basis for a shared language that guides collaborative team meetings, goal setting, professional development plans, and professional dialogue about effective practice—not just for evaluation. Teaching is a complex profession that requires thoughtful discourse about what happens at the critical point of contact between each teacher and each student (Hipp & Huffman, 2010).
- Ensure professional development of administrators *and* teachers in discerning among various levels of quality in effective teaching. Too often, administrators alone are given explicit training in how to evaluate instructional practice. Teachers can be more metacognitive about their practice when they also understand the distinction among different levels of quality.
- Develop a shared understanding among teachers and administrators of the research on growth (Dweck, 2006) and expertise (Ericsson, 2006) to eliminate the stigma that the need to improve is a liability (Mielke & Frontier, 2012). *Everyone* should be on an improvement plan.

- Develop a shared understanding among teachers and administrators of the research on deliberate practice to ensure that teachers use evidence to determine areas of weakness from which they will derive the greatest benefit from focused efforts to improve.
- Use of a variety of protocols to help teachers better understand their current practice, the next level practice, and the gap between the two in a manner that focuses on formative opportunities for feedback and growth rather than summative evaluation. Specific strategies such as instructional rounds, student surveys, and self-analysis of video of one's own practice can be extremely powerful tools for supporting professional growth (Marzano et al., 2011).
- Establish strong mentor programs that utilize specific strategies to empower new teachers to be more reflective, and effective, practitioners (Britton, Paine, Pimm, & Raizen, 2003).
- Establish strong instructional coaching programs that utilize specific strategies to empower all teachers to be more reflective, and effective, practitioners (Knight, 2011).
- Have teachers establish just a few improvement goals that focus on the more effective utilization of just a few instructional strategies each year.

Turning evaluation into a form of high-stakes summative assessment will not improve professional practice. Clearly defining what good teaching looks like, empowering teachers to engage in a loop of continuous feedback that informs deliberate practice, providing teachers with opportunities to observe and discuss expertise, establishing clear personalized plans for incremental improvement, and providing recognition to teachers as they develop expertise in various aspects of their practice are the components that should guide efforts to not only measure teacher performance but facilitate teacher growth as well.

Strategy: A Recap

In his work as a professor of public policy at the University of California, Berkeley, David Kirp has never seen a school district transformation like the one he has observed in Union City, New Jersey. In an opinion piece in the *New York Times* (2013), Kirp describes the lessons he learned after spending a year in the district doing research to gain a better understanding of how it went from being a district where "the schools were so wretched that state officials almost seized control of them" to being a thriving district. The secret, according to Kirp, is "the skills of the teacher, the engagement of the students, and the rigor of the curriculum." Union City focused on research-based strategies for effective instruction, student engagement, a teacher-mentoring program to support the use of more effective instructional techniques, and principals working as instructional leaders.

Absent researchers or reporters spending a year in a school focused on improving classroom practice, powerful initiatives like those in Union City tend not to grab headlines. The nature of the work occurs behind closed doors—through meaningful conversations among colleagues about instructional strategies, through a written reflection by a student on a formative assessment that prompts a teacher to try an alternate strategy the next day, through a thoughtfully designed comment written by a teacher on a student's paper that provides both the challenge and the support to serve as a catalyst for improved student learning.

While structural components and sampling practices in schools frequently have little or no impact on student learning, a teacher's ability to use effective instructional strategies will always have a direct impact on student learning. As a profession, we know a tremendous amount about how students learn and the instructional practices that can be used to effectively guide student learning. However, teaching is a complex profession. Transactional efforts that expect teachers to improve their ability to utilize more effective instructional strategies merely because they have been told to do so or that attempt to reduce the art of teaching to a mere checklist will fail to leverage improved practice. Prioritizing efforts and resources that empower teachers as learners on a path toward more expert use of instructional strategies is among the highest-leverage activities schools can use to affect student learning.

Connecting Strategy to the Chapter Vignettes

This chapter opened with three vignettes that illustrate varying attempts to improve student learning by using new strategies and tools. Let's reflect on what each one tells us about what works and what doesn't when trying to use this lever.

Reflections on Vignette 1: New Textbooks and New Technology.

Schools and districts can purchase new textbooks and touch-screen tablets and then use them in a structural manner that does nothing more than preserve the status quo for a student's schooling experience. To assume that new resources will result in the use of different instructional strategies is a classic leveraging error. Teachers must use these tools in the context of a rich curriculum, effective unit design, and appropriately implemented instructional strategies. Too often we've seen districts engage in curriculum review processes that are, in reality, textbook adoption or technology acquisition processes. Effective curriculum, instruction, and assessment can occur without textbooks or technology. New resources can be used in a manner that augments the quality of the curriculum and transforms student learning. Schools and districts that most effectively leverage the acquisition of new materials invest significant time, effort, and energy in establishing the professional skills and strategies, standards, assessments, and curriculum that will be used to drive students' use of those resources.

Reflections on Vignette 2: New Evaluation Tools to Ensure Greater Accountability. If the principal is deemed to be the only person in the school who can provide feedback to teachers, then we've asked principals to engage in an impossible task. If teachers perceive the sole purpose of observation to be to receive judgmental feedback, we've created a scenario in which the principal is working hard to engage in summative assessment and teachers feel frustrated by the lack of formative opportunities for growth. When no distinction is made between formative and summative processes, learners will avoid taking risks and asking questions. Constructive feedback—regardless of intent—may be perceived as judgmental rather than developmental. What typically follows is a defensive discussion about ratings rather than constructive dialogue about effective practice. If this situation persists, the opportunity to leverage supervision and evaluation as a transformational system to support reflective practice and improve teacher expertise will be sacrificed to a transactional process of following protocols and filing forms.

Reflections on Vignette 3: Collaborating on Student Achievement and Instructional Strategies. We've seen this scenario across a variety of schools and districts with high-functioning teams of teachers. This scenario is possible because teachers are working to leverage Hattie's two generalizations about classrooms that are most likely to support student learning. These teachers are willing to see the curriculum from the perspective of their students and intend to empower students to guide their own learning. If students are deficient in an area, the relevant question the teachers have asked is "What opportunities have students had to learn, develop, and monitor their progress in developing these skills?" The emphasis in this scenario is clearly on using collaboration time to transform curriculum, instruction, and assessment so that the result is improved student learning.

Connecting Strategy to the Global Prosperity Academy

This book's introduction described several ways that the Global Prosperity Academy hoped to leverage instructional strategies to improve student learning. Although the school articulated a desire to create a connected, personalized learning experience and implement a comprehensive instructional methodology to support students' abilities to solve authentic problems, the staff did not follow through on efforts to support teachers' use of new strategies. Two days of training during the summer are merely a starting point for the ongoing professional development and structured, reflective practice associated with teachers developing expertise in the use of specific instructional strategies. A transformational approach to supporting teacher expertise would have required a much deeper focus on the development and use of instructional strategies, as well as ongoing support to help teachers move from awareness to effective classroom practice.

Connecting Strategy to the Kitchen Remodeling Analogy

Strategies are central to the narrative in the kitchen analogy. A building project requires the deployment of specific strategies to attain complex, specific outcomes. Teaching is no different. A building project has different phases that require different tools. Early in the project, a backhoe is the right tool to dig the foundation; toward the end, a small hammer and finishing nails are the right tools to install the molding. Master carpenters understand how to obtain desired outcomes by having a broad range of tools to choose from, and they understand the complexity of the building process in a manner that allows them to use the right tool, at the right time, in the right way. Furthermore, the deployment of strategies is about being clear about outcomes so one can use best practices associated with attaining those outcomes. In the kitchen analogy, if the goal was to improve the structural space, the correct strategies were used to make that vision a reality. But if the goal was to improve the quality of the food, the wrong strategies were used. Building the skills of the cook would have been a dramatically more efficient and effective approach to ensuring that, in the end, the food served in the kitchen was of better quality.

Doing Less, Doing More

As we've seen with the other levers, leveraging strategy involves doing more of some high-leverage activities and behaviors, and letting go of others. Figure 4.1 summarizes key points to keep in mind as you use this lever.

Reflecting on Strategy: Questions to Ask on Monday Morning

- Is there a common language of instruction among teams? Throughout the school? Throughout the district?
- What is the amount or percentage of time I and others in our school or district spend talking about instructional strategies as *the* primary lever associated with addressing concerns or creating new learning opportunities for students?
- When looking at agendas for board, faculty, and team meetings, to what extent do agenda items and meeting minutes deal with the use of research-based instructional strategies?
- To what extent is the implementation of specific instructional strategies seen as *the goal* of initiatives in our school or district? Are adopting structural practices such as implementing a new schedule, adopting a new report card, or acquiring technology described as the goal or as a means to use more effective instructional strategies to support student learning?
- To what extent do we find ourselves waiting to implement more effective instructional strategies only after structural changes have been employed?
- What time, effort, and energy are currently being used to develop teachers' capacity to develop expertise?
- To what extent do we find teachers waiting for *students to change* rather than improving or adding to their repertoire of instructional strategies?

Questions on Strategy from the Students' Perspective

- How will the change in instructional strategy we are considering change the students' learning experience?

Figure 4.1 | Leveraging Strategy

Do Less of This	Do More of This
• Assuming that because kids were told something, they understand	• Using strategies that allow students to construct meaning around important content and build competency around important skills
• Treating students as though they are blank slates	• Using strategies that honor the fact that new knowledge is constructed on existing knowledge
• Assuming that all kids are as interested in, and are motivated to learn, the content and skills that you teach	• Striving to see learning from the perspective of each student (What is likely to be engaging? What is likely to be relevant?)
• Using rubrics as a tool to justify grades	• Using rubrics as an instructional tool to help students learn how to describe, understand, and assess quality work
• Rigidly applying models or checklists that ignore the complexities of both the art and science of teaching	• Striving for superintendents, principals, and teachers to understand the complexity and opportunity presented by comprehensive instructional frameworks as a starting point for addressing each student's learning needs
• Assuming that all instructional strategies are equally effective in improving student learning	• Acknowledging that different instructional strategies can substantially increase student achievement when deployed effectively and in the right context
• Using the same few instructional strategies	• Using a repertoire of instructional strategies that are specifically aligned to the intended outcomes for student learning
• Using collaborative time with teams of teachers to talk about structure and sample	• Using collaborative time to talk about intentional use of standards and share instructional strategies
• Principals and supervisors as the primary or exclusive users of frameworks for effective practice; only using those frameworks to render judgment	• Teachers using student surveys, analyzing video, engaging in instructional rounds to inform reflective, deliberate practice in efforts to improve

- What connections will students make between the changes in instructional strategies and their learning? Will they see the changes as responding to their needs or to teacher preference and convenience?
- How might students complete this prompt if instructional strategies are used more effectively than they have been in the past? *Before this change we used to* _____, *but now we* _____.

Look at the tables in Appendix D related to status quo, transactional, and transformational planning questions and examine the questions associated with strategy. What types of questions do you typically hear in your school or district when you and your colleagues are discussing strategy? What types of questions do you typically ask?

Lever 5: Self

Vignette 1: You Either Have It or You Don't

John has a history of not performing well in school. Now in 8th grade, he watches fellow students for whom learning seems to come easy. They can do their homework and still have time for other activities. He believes that they must have been born with the intelligence and learning abilities they possess.

John has decided he just did not receive the package at birth. In fact, trying and failing is so painful that John has decided that it is safer and far less embarrassing to act out in class, to be a clown so that other students think that he does not care. In reality, he feels cheated but cannot do anything about it, so he distracts, avoids, and rebels when nothing else works. After all, if intelligence and ability to learn are inherited, you either have it or you don't. Why try? Doing so only seems to make things worse.

Vignette 2: High-Ability Math

Washington Elementary School has had a high-ability math program for years. Students who test at the top 25 percent of their class in 3rd grade are placed in a track that will accelerate their learning through high school. These students will have the best teachers and the most opportunities to be challenged and to participate in mathematical projects and contests. Everyone knows that these are the students who will succeed in math in high school. According to the chair of the mathematics program, given their natural abilities, they deserve such exceptional opportunities.

Of course, a few will fall back as time goes on. They will be shown not to have the natural talent to keep up. But most will stay in this track and avoid the embarrassment of falling back into regular math like other students at their grade levels. Even some who really cannot keep up will find ways not to be noticed and to rely on the work of other students and, of course, nightly "support" from their parents or a tutor.

A notable fact is that once this group is formed, no additional students ever join. Washington Elementary doesn't have a process for including others because by the time newcomers could join, the students chosen as 3rd graders would be too far ahead for a student new to the program to catch up.

Vignette 3: An Amazing Turnaround

Mary has not found learning to come easily. In fact, she has had to work hard in every academic subject. Most of her teachers placed her as "low average" in her classes. Then something amazing happened.

Mary was placed in Ms. Stevens's classroom this year. Ms. Stevens took some extra time to get to know Mary as a learner in ways previous teachers had not. She determined the causes of Mary's past struggles and figured out which learning strategies seem to work best for Mary and what she is interested in. She even found a few gaps in Mary's past learning that made learning even more difficult. In addition, Ms. Stevens shared this information with Mary, meeting with her periodically to discuss the connections between the strategies Mary used and the results she achieved. They talked about the importance of persistence and using the resources and tools available to Mary to support her learning. Maybe most important, they monitored Mary's progress in response to her efforts. Ms. Stevens gave Mary frequent, clear, actionable feedback on her work and regularly listened to Mary talk about how different instructional approaches and paces of instruction helped her learning. Both Mary and Ms. Stevens adjusted their focuses and efforts in response to what they heard from each other.

Amazingly, by late fall Mary began to see her learning accelerate, and although she still needed to work hard, her efforts seemed to generate greater results than before. She began to see herself as a more capable learner and increasingly took on learning challenges to figure out how to overcome them. By spring, Mary was performing at a level comparable to students who always had been viewed as the brightest, most able learners.

Vignette 4: My Job Is to Prepare You to Not Need Me

Mr. White is not a typical teacher in his school. In fact, he often is frustrated with how he sees students being treated. For the most part, he sees his colleagues expecting, incentivizing, and sanctioning student compliance with what adults want, whether in their general behavior or their learning. He fears that this approach builds dependence in learners when the focus should be on building their capacity for independence.

He often gets pushback from colleagues who remind him that this is how school always has been. Adults are supposed to make the rules, set the expectations, and decide the incentives and sanctions. The job of students is to comply.

Mr. White sees the situation differently. He believes that the task of schools is to help learners see and develop their potential. Students should make increasingly important decisions about their learning, their choices, and their future. He worries that in a world where innovation, creativity, and flexibility are keys to success, students are not being taught to own their learning and continue to build it. He is concerned that the dependence that schools are nurturing creates a disadvantage for students who later must be independent learners and workers. He wants to change the direction and prepare students for the future they will live, not the past and present of adults.

Definition, Misconception, and Opportunity

Definition: *Self includes the set of beliefs that teachers and students have about their capacity to be effective.*

What students and staff believe to be true about the nature and nurture of learning can have a profound impact on student learning (Dweck, 2000; Howard, 1995; Rosenthal & Jacobson, 1968). Research on teacher efficacy speaks to the importance of teachers' belief in their capacity to address the learning needs of different students. Research on student efficacy speaks to the amount of effort and level of persistence students will give to their schoolwork based on beliefs about their capacity and the nature of the task, use of effective strategies, and leveraging resources available to them.

Misconception: *Educators' and students' underlying beliefs about the nature and nurture of intelligence are aligned to the statement that all students can learn.*

Just because it says "all students can learn" in a strategic plan or a mission statement does not mean that this concept is ingrained in educators' belief systems. Until we have confronted and untangled the complex web of thinking that underlies fixed versus developmental beliefs about intelligence (see Dweck, 2006; Nisbett, 2009), understand how factors such as stereotype threat can affect student learning (Steele et al., 2002), and challenge assumptions about whether innate talent or effective effort determines each student's trajectory (Ericsson, 2006; Howard, 1995), we cannot necessarily expect that educators hold and act upon the belief that intelligence is malleable and intellect can be increased. Furthermore, it is often assumed that nothing can be done to address students' perceptions of themselves as learners; there is a reluctance to acknowledge, let alone influence, what is inside the "black box" of their minds. This assumption results in the misconception that characteristics such as motivation and effort are fixed rather than malleable.

Opportunity: *Our mental models about how teaching relates to learning capacity have largely gone unexamined.*

What we believe to be true about the nature and nurture of learning has a profound impact on decisions we make about the strategies, standards, samples, and structures we will use or develop for ourselves, our students, and our schools. It also holds the key to significantly increasing learning— especially for students who do not have individuals in their households who have already accessed the benefits of formal education. Currently schools do little to encourage open, honest dialogue about how our mental models of the relationship among concepts of intelligence, effort, talent, and development can limit or accelerate our capacity to improve student learning. Ensuring that students have a productive disposition toward learning is such a critical factor to student success that it cannot be left to chance. In fact, we argue that developing and nurturing this disposition should be among the primary areas of focus for schools. The potential of strategically tending to students' beliefs about their capacity to learn can be surprisingly simple yet have a profound impact on student learning (Yeager & Walton, 2011).

Developing Independence by Leveraging Conceptions of Self

Over the years, research has confirmed the importance of self as a key element in student learning. Butler and Winne (1995) synthesized the theory on feedback and self-regulated learning and came to this conclusion:

> Theoreticians seem unanimous—the most effective learners are self-regulating. In academic contexts, self-regulation is a style of engaging with tasks in which students exercise a suite of powerful skills: setting goals for upgrading knowledge; deliberating about strategies to select those that balance progress toward goals against unwanted costs; and, as steps are taken and the task evolves, monitoring the accumulating effects of their engagement. (p. 245)

In a synthesis of the impact of social-psychological interventions on student learning, David Yeager and Gregory Walton (2011) explain how small interventions with students can have a significant impact on student learning. Yeager and Walton describe randomized, controlled interventions in which students did the following:

- Wrote a brief essay about how something they are learning in science class could be applied to their lives (Hulleman & Harackiewicz, 2009).
- Wrote about how their future selves might be academically successful (Oyserman, Bybee, & Terry, 2006).
- Wrote about values that are important to them (Cohen, Garcia, Apfel, & Master, 2006; Cohen, Garcia, Purdie-Vaughns, Apfel, & Brzustoski, 2009).
- Explained to younger students that intelligence is malleable (Aronson, Fried, & Good, 2002).

By design, students were given wide latitude in how they approached these tasks. Each of these interventions required a minimal amount of time to administer but produced significant positive results in student achievement. How can this be? As Yeager and Walton explain, how these interventions work may seem as mysterious as the forces at play that allow thousands of pounds of metal and wire to take flight when formed as an airplane. Critical elements—air currents and aerodynamic forces that provide lift to an airplane, and confidence, efficacy, and beliefs about intelligence in students—cannot be seen but, given the right conditions, can produce dramatic results. Specifically, Yeager and Walton (2011) argue the following:

> As a consequence, even a seemingly small intervention but one that removes a critical barrier to learning can produce substantial effects on academic outcomes. At a broader level, this theoretical foundation underscores the fundamental inappropriateness of viewing social-psychological interventions as silver bullets; rather than operating in isolation, such interventions rearrange forces in a complex system. (p. 275)

The concept of *self* as a lever to powerfully drive learning rests on the relationships among five learner characteristics—*motivation, engagement, self-efficacy, ownership of learning,* and *independence*—and the power they hold to create highly proficient, consistently motivated learners (Rickabaugh, 2012). Typically, we think about each of these characteristics separately or at best as loosely connected. For example, we might think about how to motivate learners without making the direct connection in our strategy to engaging them in their learning. We might look for ways to build self-efficacy in our students but fail to see how this effort can also promote ownership for learning. We can also miss the cumulative impact of all of these efforts to build learner independence. When we fail to make these connections, we risk focusing on each characteristic in isolation, hoping that somehow they will lead to learners who are persistent, independent problem solvers and accomplished self-regulators, able to focus on what they need to learn and to do so without depending on external structures and support.

When we tap the synergistic power of these characteristics, we can make a determinative difference in the learning and long-term success of our learners. These are key leveraging advantages. Nurturing *motivation* gives us access to the attention and potential energy of the learner, regardless of whether the motivation is inherent or ignited by an external source. When acted upon, the latent potential of motivation becomes *engagement*; engaged learners participate in activities, attempt to understand, and act on the challenge or learning task. Although engagement in learning tasks and activities can generate learning, it also presents opportunities for students to see the connection between their efforts and strategies and the learning results they experience. Learners further increase their sense of self as a learner as they experience the power to have an impact on their environment, overcome challenges, and influence their own success—in short, to build *self-efficacy*. The results generated from employing this growing understanding of self as a key element to influence environment and events become an extension of the learner and create a sense of *ownership of learning*—a key to long-term learning success. The experience of this set of relationships positions learners to employ increasingly effective strategies to build their learning competence; to decide among the available options and opportunities those that will best serve their learning interests; and to establish structures, routines, and mental models to increase the efficiency of their learning endeavors.

The cumulative impact of developing self-motivation, engaged learning, self-efficacy, and ownership of learning equips learners with many of the crucial tools to achieve *independence*, which is the lifelong outcome that formal education seeks to achieve. This process transforms students from compliant consumers of prepackaged content and concepts to committed creators of knowledge, insight, and learning opportunity.

When we leverage the power of self by placing learners at the center of our work and focusing on the connections and development of the five key learning elements, we endow learners with the power to increasingly become owners of, coworkers in, and codesigners of their learning. When we tap the potential of self as a lever for learning , we give our learners the power to choose, influence, change, and grow without having to depend on educators, parents, bosses, and others in positions of authority to direct their learning activities and life paths.

Our effectiveness in employing the concept of self to build and tap motivation, engagement, self-efficacy, ownership, and independence requires an understanding of the dimensions of each element, how they contribute to learning, the strategies we can use, and how each element can prepare learners for the next stage toward full learning independence. In the following sections we examine each element and explain how educators can employ and leverage it to build a sense of self and to position the learner for the next level of understanding and learning power.

Using Conception of Self to Build Motivation

By definition, motivation is the presence of an emotional or a psychological inclination or attraction to a task, an idea, a challenge, or an understanding. Interest, curiosity, sense of challenge, and desire to understand are among the behavioral signs indicating the presence of motivation. Particularly related to education, learner motivation "refers to a student's willingness, need, desire, and compulsion to participate in, and be successful in, the learning process" (Bomia et al., in Brewster & Fager, 2000, p. 4).

Motivation as a Contributor to Learning

Motivation is a personal experience and a key entry point to stimulate learning. Most experts divide motivation into two forms: intrinsic and extrinsic. *Intrinsic motivation* includes the desire to learn, understand, make sense, find meaning and purpose, gain mastery, and work autonomously (Pink, 2009). *Extrinsic motivation* comes from external rewards such as grades, stickers, adult approval, and other things not directly related to the object of learning.

Intrinsic motivation is more likely to tap positive emotions and prior learning and has been shown to lead to better recall and retention (Lumsden, 1994; Voke, 2002). Conversely, when extrinsic motivation is used to stimulate learning, learners typically understand less, retain less, and do not show lasting commitment to learning, consistent with our argument that the farther away from self each lever is, the less power it possesses. In fact, when extrinsic rewards are withdrawn, they can actually undermine future learning (Kohn, 1995). The key understanding for educators is to focus on strategies that build intrinsic motivation in learners to retain their natural sense of curiosity to learn, rather than undermine this force by incenting them to comply or achieve an external reward, such as a grade.

Building Motivation Through the Lever of Self

Ames (1992) describes three classroom conditions that can tap learner motivation: (1) tasks and learning activities that are relevant and meaningful, (2) rewards and assessment, and (3) autonomy and learner choice.

The most direct way to tap learner motivation is to know and consult the individual and design tasks and learning activities in response. Learners vary in terms of interests, areas of curiosity, drive to understand, and openness to challenge. By tapping natural or inherent areas of motivation, we can harness learner attention and effort for learning.

Educators can also design activities to stimulate interest, curiosity, and challenge using intriguing questions, interesting observations, unexpected events, and surprising facts. For example, a child may not demonstrate a natural motivation to solve math problems from the book, but relating the same mathematical challenge to the student's favorite baseball team can stimulate intrinsic motivation.

A second approach to building motivation is to use rewards that help students connect their efforts to progress on key skills and understanding (Ames, 1992). However, to be effective as a learning motivation tool, the extrinsic incentive reward needs to be withdrawn as soon as intrinsic motivation has been stimulated and can be sustained.

Lastly, devolving some control and authority in the classroom to learners has been supported across a number of studies as an effective way to develop learners' intrinsic motivation (Ames, 1992). Learners who do not have a voice or a choice in what happens in class are more likely to be unmotivated. In this situation, school is something that is done *to* them (Kohn, 2010). However, there are important strategies to consider when creating greater learner voice and autonomy in the classroom. For example, learners must be allowed to make choices that are meaningful and also to generate options, not simply choose from those given to them by adults. In addition, learners should be given the opportunity to make decisions with their peers, not only individually. It is important to note that the goal is not learner-run schools—the educator still plays a critical role in codeveloping tasks and guiding the learner (Kohn, 2010).

How Motivation Leads to Engagement

Some of the motivation and engagement literature treats these two concepts—motivation and engagement—as one and the same. However, there is an important distinction. Russell, Ainley, and Frydenberg (2005) provide the picture of a motivated but disengaged learner, citing a study of middle school students who "recorded high, positive scores on a scale concerning their own motivation situation, but indicated that they found only a low level of interest in their classroom work" (p. 3). In this context, the lever of self is present but not aligned with the intended learning focus.

The connection between motivation and engagement is tight and progressive. "Motivation is about energy and direction, the reasons for behavior, why we do what we do. Engagement describes energy in action, the connection between person and activity" (Russell et al., 2005, p. 1).

Learners are engaged when they act on tasks that are interesting, challenging, and important to them—all elements residing in the conceptualization of self as a driver of behavior, including learning. It follows that if learners are motivated intrinsically, engagement is likely to follow. The presence of motivation makes engagement easier to nurture because the emotional and psychological inclination is already present, but the teacher may have to use strategy as a lever to ensure that the engagement generated is in the direction of the intended learning. The progression from motivation to engagement is generally a matter of stimulating and supporting learners to put their motivation into learning-aligned action.

Using Conception of Self to Build Engagement

Engagement occurs when learners make a psychological investment in learning (Newmann, in Voke, 2002) and take pride in learning and understanding for their own benefit, not just for grades. Active learner engagement inspires persistence even in the face of difficulty (Schlechty, 2001). As noted, engagement is motivation in action.

Engagement as a Contributor to Learning

Engagement typically is categorized as behavioral, emotional, or cognitive in nature. Each type of engagement can support learning if the activities involved are aligned with key learning goals and contribute to understanding, meaning making, and mastery. Learning is more likely to be supported by a focus on the process necessary for goal mastery rather than product outcomes, because products are more likely to be a *by-product* of learning, not learning itself (Ames, 1992).

Learners who are engaged in school tend to have better attendance, exhibit fewer behavior problems, and are more likely to complete learning tasks (Schlechty, 2011). Learners following these patterns are less likely to be removed from classrooms and other environments where teaching and learning are occurring and are more likely to pay attention and make the effort necessary to absorb academic content and build intended skills.

Building Engagement Through the Lever of Self

The quality of the work we present to learners can influence the levels and strength of their engagement (Schlechty, 2002). Schlechty proposes the following 10 characteristics of work that can enhance quality and support student engagement:

- Content and substance
- Organization of knowledge
- Product focus
- Clear and compelling product standards
- Safe environment
- Affirmation of performance
- Affiliation
- Novelty and variety
- Choice
- Authenticity

When students can connect the content and substance of what they are learning to their interests and goals and find meaning in what they are learning, engagement grows. When the way in which the content or skills presented for learning is organized makes sense to the learner, engaging in the work becomes an easier task. When students see and value what will be the product of their learning and it is accompanied by standards of quality in which they can take pride, they are more likely to choose to invest their time and effort. Equally powerful, learning in a safe context where quality performance at the student's level of learning development is recognized and affirmed can be compelling. When students are offered choice in what and how they will learn and the way in which learning is presented includes an appropriate variety of tasks and activities and includes surprises, unusual aspects, and fun, learning becomes an invitation to engage and enjoy. Finally, when the work of learning offers the potential of "real-world" outcomes and can be done while working with friends and classmates, it can be irresistible. Interestingly, each of these elements derives its power from the connection it has to the conception of self as a key lever for learning.

Strong, Silver, and Robinson (1995) surveyed learners about the type of work they find engaging. Learners reported that the work they found most engaging allowed creativity, sparked curiosity, presented opportunities to work with others, produced feelings of and held the potential for success, and was challenging. Conversely, they pointed to work that was repetitive, was forced by others, and required no thinking as being disengaging. Keller (2000) argues that four conditions are necessary for a person to be fully motivated and engaged: attention, relevance, confidence, and satisfaction—the ARCS model. Again, each of the four conditions is tightly connected to self as a powerful lever to nurture engagement that leads to learning.

Given the tight linkage between intrinsic motivation and engagement, it is no surprise that the literature poses many of the same strategies to build engagement as it does to tap learner motivation. Additionally, Heather Voke (2002) summarizes the research, noting that engagement can be built through curriculum and goals that are appropriate and achievable for each learner, constructive and frequent feedback, and safe environments that build a sense of community.

How Engagement Contributes to Self-Efficacy

When we are so engrossed in a task that we lose track of time and find it difficult to stop, we are experiencing what is known as "flow," which can be thought of in terms of learners being fully engaged. Knowing that the activity is doable is one of the seven characteristics that Csikszentmihalyi (2004) describes as being present when a person is in the state of flow. This is a key factor in self-efficacy, and the overlap demonstrates the interconnectedness of engagement and self-efficacy.

When learners are engaged in learning with focused, sustained effort on a task just outside their current skill level, engagement often results. When learners experience success in such activities, increased self-efficacy often follows. Learners begin to see the connection between effort and results.

In contrast, Russell and her colleagues (2005) describe learned helplessness as a form of disengagement. "Students who experience repeated failure may come to believe that nothing they can do will alter the situation, the opposite of self-efficacy."

Using Conception of Self to Build Efficacy

Self-efficacy is generally described as a set of beliefs about the learner's capacity to marshal and maintain the efforts necessary to achieve a selected goal (Bandura, 1986, 1991). In the case of academic self-efficacy, it is the learners' belief that they can control their academic outcomes by the strategies they employ, the effort they exert, and the resources they engage (Wigfield & Wagner, 2005). This definition closely parallels the lever of *self* as the entry point for efficacy and the lever of *strategy* as efficacy employed.

Self-Efficacy as a Contributor to Learning

The presence or absence of strong self-efficacy often determines whether learners will engage in challenging tasks in which the outcome of the work is not certain. A low level of self-efficacy can result in learners refusing to try, believing that they are not inherently capable of succeeding; for these learners, refusing to try is preferable to feelings that result from failure. It can also lead learners to prematurely abandon efforts that require struggle, because they believe that if success is not *immediately* attainable, it probably is not *ultimately* attainable. Conversely, a high level of self-efficacy leads learners to persist in the face of challenge, to continually try different approaches and strategies to overcome obstacles, and to search for resources that will provide leverage and advantages necessary to achieve success. Without question, the beliefs learners hold about self are a determinant of whether they will engage in challenging tasks from which learning can result.

Associated with self-efficacy is the concept discussed earlier related to fixed versus developable intelligence. Learners who are convinced that intelligence is something one either does or does not have will often avoid learning tasks in which success is not ensured to get around the possibility of being shown not to be "smart." Conversely, learners who see intelligence as being malleable and developable are more likely to see challenging tasks as a means to learn, understand, and develop skills needed for success and will engage despite the risk that success may not be immediately forthcoming (Dweck, 2006). Again, the conceptualization of self wields significant influence on whether learners will invest the effort necessary to generate learning.

Building Efficacy Through the Lever of Self

Because self-efficacy is strongly associated with the beliefs of the learner, making changes requires a change in both behavior and mental models. A well-known study by Carol Dweck involved helping middle school learners develop general study skills but also to think about their brain as a muscle like any other muscle, in that improvement requires exercise and practice just like in athletics or any other skill-based activity (Dweck, 2007). The result of even this level of change in perspective and belief led the learners involved to perform significantly higher than classmates who engaged only in learning related to study skills. Once again, beliefs about and understanding of the potential power of self as a lever are crucial to learning.

Goal setting has been demonstrated to be a useful strategy in building learners' self-efficacy (Schunk, 1991). Close-at-hand goals with specific
performance standards help learners to understand and judge progress
and then translate that to their sense of self. Additionally, helping learners
identify and use learning strategies raises self-efficacy. Learners who perceive that they are comprehending material feel enhanced efficacy. Watching peers complete a task can serve as a model for other learners, helping
them to develop confidence that they, too, can complete the task. Explicit
feedback to learners regarding the role that effort, strategy, and employed
resources are playing in their success is also helpful. Feedback that pertains
to both skill and effort particularly can build efficacy (Schunk, 1991).

Helping learners to see that effort, persistence, strategy, and good use of
resources can increase their learning in ways that they control can make a
key difference in the level of effort learners will give and their willingness to
persist and to identify and try alternative approaches.

How Self-Efficacy Contributes to Ownership of Learning

The stronger the sense of self-efficacy, the more likely it is that learners will
be able to succeed in the face of challenge and even initial failure. Learners
with strong self-efficacy understand the connection between their efforts
and actions and the learning results they experience. When efficacious
learners work diligently to achieve a goal or learn a skill, they not only feel a
sense of accomplishment but also understand that the success they achieve
is theirs. This insight also allows learners to see their accomplishments
as being under their control and, as a result, under their ownership. Zimmerman, Bandura, and Martinez-Pons indicate that "self-regulated learners
exhibit a high sense of efficacy in their capabilities" (1992, p. 664). It follows
that efficacy naturally contributes to learners' ability to own their learning.
In this context, self as the lever for and source of accomplishment leads to
feelings of ownership for the learning that results.

Using Conception of Self to Build Ownership of Learning

Learners with a sense of ownership see their learning as something over
which they have control, that cannot be taken from them, and in which they
can take pride. Ownership of learning transfers responsibility for success

from others to the learner. Consequently, the learner values the experience and the result of effort. Self in this context plays a central role and offers key leverage to build ownership of learning.

Ownership as a Contributor to Learning

At the core of the relationship between ownership and learning is the shift from learning as a compliance activity to learning as a commitment-driven activity. When learners see learning as a process in which they must exhibit compliance behaviors, they are more likely to do the minimum to satisfy expectations and avoid negative consequences. Conversely, when they see learning as being consistent with their commitment to expand their knowledge and their ability to influence their environment, learning takes on a different hue. The question no longer is "How much must I do?" but, rather, "What do I need to do to accomplish my goals and build my competence?" This shift in perspective taps the leverage of self as a key driver for learning. Whereas the traditional model of schooling depends heavily on compliance behavior, unleashing a sense of ownership for learning can dramatically improve learner performance, even within the current system.

Building Ownership of Learning Through the Lever of Self

One of the most direct ways to build ownership for learning is to offer learners choice and control related to their learning (Kohn, 1993). The areas of choice and control need to be consistent with learning goals. Obviously, the presence of choice and control gives voice and power to the lever of self. This statement does not imply that learners necessarily are given unlimited choice over what they are to learn but, rather, that they are given a choice over how they might approach their learning. It is important to recognize that this strategy is also a part of building motivation, engagement, and self-efficacy.

Inviting learners to define challenges, design approaches, and carry out learning activities can also effectively build ownership for outcomes. It is interesting to note that this approach also allows learners to design in meaning, purpose, and mastery as the learning challenge takes shape (Stefanou, Perencevich, DiCintio, & Turner, 2004). This point was made clear by a group of middle school students who were studying freshwater marine life in a school near Lake Michigan. Instead of showing a video or asking students to read preselected text regarding varieties of fish or the ecosystem in which they live, the teacher took her students on a field trip to a nearby marine life exhibition facility. Upon arrival students were challenged to find something they would like to learn about and collect as much information as they could during the visit. After returning to the school, the students developed a description of what they wanted to learn, information related to the topic they collected during the visit, and a plan to become an "expert" on their topic. Next, they were asked to plan what they could do with their new knowledge to help others learn from their expertise. Not surprisingly, the students not only were excited but also reported giving far more effort to their learning than usual and beamed with pride when they explained how they used their new knowledge to teach classmates and younger students. Some even volunteered at the freshwater marine facility to share their learning with visitors.

Another useful strategy is to invite learner participation in goal setting. Offering learners the opportunity to be an influential partner in goal setting often leads to more ownership. When this is extended to include participating in setting broader criteria for success, learners typically will set a challenging bar and exert more effort to achieve (Osberg, 1997). A teacher whose classroom we visited routinely conferences with her students before they begin the process of learning new skills or units of study. They discuss any options available to students about what and how they will learn, using established learning standards. They talk about what the learning will involve; the learning activities and strategies they will use, including the teacher's instruction; and what students already know that can help them with their efforts. The students and teacher jointly decide specifically what the learning goal will be and how students will demonstrate that they have learned the skill or content involved. Not surprisingly, engagement in the classroom is routinely high. Even more important, learners in this classroom learn at a faster pace, are more independent in their learning, take greater ownership for the learning resulting from their efforts, and score amazingly well on standardized tests.

How Ownership of Learning Contributes to Learning Independence

Ownership for learning rests on and draws from the previous three elements that leverage self—motivation, engagement, and self-efficacy—and adds the dimension of seeing learning as something that is proprietary and cannot be taken away. Combined, these elements give the learner flexibility, competence, confidence, and power to learn without the supports of formal education structures. In short, ownership for learning positions the learner to make decisions, allocate energy, and develop meaning and insight unique to the learner—important activities that lead to independence as a learner. In essence, the learning is tapping the lever of self to focus, build, and protect learning.

Using Conception of Self to Build Learning Independence

The ability to learn independently gives learners unique powers and advantages in school and in life. Independent learners take responsibility for their own motivation and growth. They are led by curiosity, the drive to understand and make sense of their environment—all elements of leveraging *self*. They understand and appreciate their ability to meet and overcome learning challenges through the application of effective strategies, persistence, and marshaling of necessary resources. Independent learners treat their learning as owners treat other prized possessions by protecting, maintaining, and updating as needed. Independent learners understand when they need to add to their learning or to abandon beliefs and assumptions that are no longer useful. Additionally, they engage the resources, support, and instruction necessary to ensure that they actually gain the learning they seek.

Independence as a Contributor to Learning

As long as learners are dependent on others to tell them when, what, and how to learn, they will never completely take charge of their learning fate and future. They will never gain the advantages that accompany proactive learning and the ability to anticipate needs and opportunities to gain new knowledge that will serve them well in life and career. Conversely, learners who have reached a level of independence that allows them to anticipate the need to learn and to choose the learning path best suited to them possess greater chances for success.

Learners who are able to learn independently gain the flexibility to learn on demand as circumstances dictate rather than defaulting to what someone else directs, thus leveraging their sense of self to guide behavior rather than depending on others. Learning in this context often is richer because it is sought, not assigned. It is more focused because it serves a purpose. And it is retained because it is applied to solve a problem, gain a needed skill, or enrich an aspect of life.

In the workplace, independent learning skills and orientation also give workers an important advantage to accelerate careers and ensure continued employment opportunities. When workers anticipate the need to gain new skills and competencies, unlearn and abandon practices that no longer apply, or add value and offer these gifts in the workplace, they distinguish themselves as being of special value to employers, companies, and organizations. These same skills position entrepreneurs and public servants to build and lead excellent organizations, provide quality services, and produce innovative products.

Building Learning Independence Through the Lever of Self

The task of building learning independence starts at the other end of the development continuum, with the element of motivation. When learners understand how to channel their interest and curiosity, they gain the ability to motivate themselves. When learners act on their interests and motivation, they begin to understand the power they possess to support their learning. When learners understand the relationship among effort, strategy, persistence, and use of resources to meet learning challenges, they gain the power to control what they learn. And when learners begin to own their learning, they gain a prized possession to protect, build, and maintain for a lifetime.

More specifically, learners can build independence by employing a variety of strategies. Similar to building ownership over learning, giving learners choices and encouraging them to reflect on their interests and preferences and how they play a role in the choices they make can build independence. Also, giving learners increasing opportunities to work in groups where they are encouraged to learn from each other rather than centering their attention on educators or other adults can move learners toward independence. Setting learning goals can be useful to the process of building independence when learners are active participants in reflecting on what is to be learned, evaluating where their learning is currently, and deciding what would be realistic and achievable for them. Furthermore, exposing learners to a growing array of original, authentic texts that encourage them to analyze and draw conclusions about real-world, connected content can build independent competence and confidence. Similarly, encouraging learners to keep learning journals can help them to reflect on what worked for them and how they might employ the same or another strategy even more effectively in the future (Mynard & Sorflaten, 2002).

Also effective in building independence is a gradual-release strategy that gives learners progressively more voice in and control of their learning. This strategy in its fully developed form is employed in Finland, where learners, beginning in 10th grade, plan their learning goals and activities and monitor their own progress (Tucker, 2011).

Taken together, these insights and skills position learners to become independent—whether they are completing projects, accomplishing extended tasks, addressing and solving complex problems, or developing new ideas and approaches to serve a need. Regardless of the specific strategy, we need to give learners opportunities to learn independently, first with our coaching and guidance and later without our immediate presence and support. Learners will make mistakes and missteps, but these experiences are also part of the process of learning to be independent.

Starting with Self: All Learning Is Personal

The dominant system of education in the United States relies on organizing learners into groups, typically sorted by age or other characteristics, and exposing them to instruction, models, examples, and other stimuli to generate learning. The underlying assumption associated with this practice is that learning occurs best, or at least most efficiently, when students are grouped in batches.

Yet we know that exposure to the same stimuli may result in learning for some students but have no impact on others. This reality creates a significant and costly built-in inefficiency in the educational system. Such inefficiency was not a problem when the economic and social needs of the United States required that only a minority of the population be educated at high levels. It was also tolerable when districts could afford to allocate large portions of their education resources to remediation and special education programs and services that were only marginally effective.

So how can we employ this focus on self, or the learner, to dramatically improve learning at scale in the education system? Not surprisingly, our first efforts must be focused on developing a deep, rich understanding of the characteristics, learning preferences, interests, learning history, and readiness of the learner. Without this understanding we cannot hope to increase the frequency and predictability of engagement and connection that learners experience with what they are to learn.

Conversely, armed with this information and the active participation of the learner, we can dramatically increase the predictability of our efforts to engage learners in ways that result in connections, interactions, context building, and new learning. In fact, we can work with students to design and construct a learning path that accelerates progress and deepens understanding for each of them.

Not surprisingly, this frame for thinking about learners and learning represents a fundamental shift from traditional, legacy approaches in education. In this frame, the learner is not a receptacle to be filled with information, knowledge, and skills. Rather, as we discussed in Chapter 4, learners are a resource to inform, accelerate, and enrich their own learning. Individual learners are seen as key resources to be understood and tapped to design strategies and experiences that will result in learning—learning that has meaning and purpose, and that leads to mastery and includes appropriate autonomy.

Additionally, when learning conditions and challenges indicate it is appropriate, this frame allows us to tap learners as a resource to support *each other's* learning. We might position students as collaborators in a learning challenge to bring more perspectives and ideas to the work. Or we might position students as peer tutors to tap the power of novice learners as teachers to solidify their new understandings while sharing the insights and discoveries that often are evident to the novice but may be long forgotten by the expert. We know that when learning is new and fresh, learners are better able to recall and describe the learning strategies and processes that yielded results. Meanwhile, having to explain and describe new learning can further embed understandings and lead to even greater depth of learning for the novice.

Furthermore, thinking of learners as a resource positions us to consistently gain feedback on the effectiveness of the learning experiences we design and the instruction we provide. After all, unless our actions make a positive difference to the learner, they are not effective. If we do not know what is working from the perspective of the learner, we cannot calibrate and otherwise adjust in ways that improve the effectiveness of our instruction and the predictability of the learning outcomes we seek.

The synergy created by this shift in the ways we think about learners and their roles holds a powerful implication. In the frame of learners as actors and contributors to their own learning and the learning environment, we see the promise of unleashing the greatest untapped resources in schools today. This approach starts with the learner. This strategy by itself promises to dramatically increase learning and educational productivity in ways that more financial support and other structural elements likely will never achieve.

So what does all of this mean? If we hope to dramatically improve learning quality and accelerate the rate at which learners progress, we must start by designing learning environments around what will be effective for the learner—and we must include the learner as a resource and an active partner in this work. We know from research conducted decades ago that this approach holds the promise to make a dramatic difference in learning for virtually all types of learners (Bloom, 1984).

Self: A Recap

In this section we presented the argument that conception of self is a crucial factor in determining student learning engagement and success. Conception of self determines whether learners will invest in a challenging learning experience, persist when the work becomes difficult, and feel a sense of ownership after they've completed the task. How students see themselves as learners is not only related to short and long-term academic goals, it is also related to how they will define success and pursue goals throughout their lives.

We have also argued that the concept of self related to learning is crucial to efforts to change learning systems to increase learner engagement, commitment, and performance. Failure to take into account and leverage this factor in school improvement and redesign efforts predictably will result in limited, if any, positive results despite the level of activity, investment, or expectation. There are many levers we can pull in our attempts to improve learning for students, but none are more powerful than this one.

Fortunately, there is much we can do to build and sustain healthy student conceptions of self that will empower them to invest, persist, and prevail in a variety of learning situations. Each of these strategies and efforts begins with a commitment to take the student into account when deciding learning goals, paths, and expected outcomes.

Connecting Standards to the Chapter Vignettes

The four vignettes that opened this chapter illustrate varying perceptions by students and teachers of the importance of self as a lever for improved performance. Let's consider what each demonstrates about this critical element in teaching and learning.

Reflections on Vignette 1: You Either Have It or You Don't. The student in the case study sees academic intelligence as something that is bestowed on people rather than something that can be developed and strengthened over time with persistent, effective effort. Consequently, he concludes that his best strategy is to protect himself from the embarrassment and shame of failure by avoiding work and acting out. What appears to be laziness or apathy is often a student making strategic decisions to preserve self-perception: *If spending a lot of time studying is proof that I am not smart, then I will save time and face by pretending not to care.* His perception of himself as a learner and his misperception that other students don't need to try hard to be successful need to be directly addressed if he is to be reengaged. He would be well served by teachers who help him focus his energy on incrementally building skills and developing a set of useful learning strategies rather than avoiding engagement and failing to build learning capacity. He would be best served by internalizing Jeff Howard's (1990) core message in his work on student efficacy: *Smart isn't something you are; smart is something you get. If you are not successfully learning, it is simply because we haven't found an effective strategy yet.* Furthermore, he would be best served by teachers who clearly and consistently communicate the mantra *This is important. You can do this. I won't give up on you.* A transactional mission statement that says "We believe that all students can learn" means very little unless the school employs specific strategies to avoid unintentionally communicating erroneous messages to students that there are exceptions to this statement, or when all the adults in the school do not aggressively intervene when they see students who do not believe the statement to be true.

Reflections on Vignette 2: High-Ability Math. Students showing high levels of achievement early in their schooling often are provided with affirmation, additional resources, and additional opportunities to learn. Not surprisingly, these opportunities continually build on the students' early promise. Consequently, their achievement can become the equivalent of a self-fulfilling prophecy. Meanwhile, other students who do not come to school with early external supports or those whose interest or effort in a particular discipline or domain develops later in their schooling experience are left without the opportunities and resources that could lead to full development of their potential. Furthermore, when large groups of students are tracked early on in a school's or district's structure, sampling becomes a lever that affirms a portion of students but demotivates others.

Reflections on Vignette 3: An Amazing Turnaround. Mary's amazing turnaround grew out of several factors that are key to nurturing competence in students. Her teacher took the time to really get to know and build a relationship with Mary. She made an effort to understand Mary as a learner and coached Mary to seek out useful strategies and develop good learning habits, and she provided instruction that was relevant to and at a pace appropriate to Mary's readiness to learn.

Reflections on Vignette 4: My Job Is to Prepare You to Not Need Me. Mr. White positioned himself as an educator whose first responsibility is to build each learner's capacity to be independent. His focus was on moving learners from a transactional, compliance-driven approach to a transformational approach in which students were effectively challenged and taught the skills necessary to guide their own learning. He understood that learners will not always have someone to tell them what, when, and how to learn and work. He understood that student responsibility for learning is not a wish he had for each student; rather, it is a skill set to be taught. In his view, his role as a teacher was to provide instructional opportunities that prepare students to tend to their own success, or to see themselves as their own best teacher.

Connecting Self to the Global Prosperity Academy

The vision of the Global Prosperity Academy presented in the introduction to this book included lofty aspirations about how student learning would be enriched and enhanced compared with the learning that typically occurs in other school environments. Unfortunately, the steps taken and the designs adopted did not substantially change the learning experiences of students when compared with their experiences under the previous structure. In essence, the school did not leverage students' central role in the learning equation so that it aligned with the vision.

The power of changing and leveraging the role of the learner to improve individual and system performance has been repeatedly reinforced for Jim in his recent work in the area of personalized learning and exploring ways to build scalable, sustainable systems of personalized learning. At first it may seem counterintuitive to begin to create a higher-capacity approach to education by starting with the learner and building the system around what the learner needs. This approach suggests building the capacity of the learner and employing the other levers to provide the supports necessary to sustain and scale opportunities for all learners to grow and achieve at high levels.

The "start with the learner" approach can give us a new perspective on the work we do as educators. It is not just to teach the curriculum or to set high standards for students to achieve. It is not about grouping students by select characteristics and instructing to those aspects of their person. Nor is it about creating structures that will mold the behaviors of those within it. Creating the educational system we need requires us to employ all of the levers, but to be successful we must start with—and keep at the center—students and their needs, potential, capacity, and aspirations.

Connecting Self to the Kitchen Remodeling Analogy

The role of self, like the other levers, is relevant to the analogy of a kitchen remodel. Changing the structure, layout, and quality of tools and appliances available improved the environment, but without changes in the approach, capacity, and role of the cook, the outcomes did not change. Changes in these other factors can create the potential and opportunity for improvement in the outcome, but just as the cook remains central to the quality of the food prepared, so the learner remains the central element in ensuring the highest possible outcomes for student learning.

Doing Less, Doing More

As we've seen with the other four levers, leveraging self requires educators to do less of certain things and more of others. Figure 5.1 presents both sides of the equation.

Reflecting on Conceptions of Self: Questions to Ask on Monday Morning

- Is there a common language and consistent understanding of the role of self in accelerating learning and deepening understanding among staff teams? In the school? In the district?

Figure 5.1 | Leveraging Self

Do Less of This	Do More of This
• Assuming that because kids are compliant they are committed to learning	• Focusing on nurturing factors that will lead students to commit to learn for their own uses and purposes
• Treating students as though they are solely receptacles for our knowledge and wisdom	• Using students as resources by drawing on their past experiences, imagination, curiosity, and knowledge to build and expand learning capacity and success
• Assuming that all students learn in the same way and at the same rate as classmates and others of the same age	• Designing learning paths with students that accommodate the ways in which they can learn best and at a pace that is responsive to their needs
• Implying that intelligence is a fixed characteristic	• Affirming and teaching that intelligence is malleable and involves hard work, and the right strategy improves everyone's understanding and skills
• Providing praise that affirms fixed abilities ("You must be really smart.")	• Providing praise that affirms effort and strategy ("What an insightful answer! How did you come up with that?")
• Relying on grades as a sole means of communicating learning progress	• Developing clear learning goals and a variety of means to demonstrate and communicate that learning has occurred
• Assuming that the current level of students' achievement is a reflection of their potential to learn	• Finding ways for every student to build the skills and develop the strategies necessary to lift performance and succeed in learning
• Assuming that learning is something that will happen to students as a group	• Understanding that although learning may occur in a group or social context, all learning ultimately is a personal experience; and that unless students make a personal connection with what they are to learn, learning does not occur
• Standards used exclusively by teachers	• Students empowered to use standards to clarify where they can invest efforts to improve

- What is the amount or percentage of time I or others in our school or district spend talking about students' concept of self as *the* primary lever associated with addressing concerns or creating new learning opportunities for students?
- When looking at agendas and minutes for board, faculty, and team meetings, to what extent do agenda items and meeting minutes reveal the use and development of the conception of self as a key lever for lifting the level and improving the richness of learning?
- To what extent is a focus on developing learner efficacy, commitment, ownership, and independence seen as *the goal* of initiatives in our school or district? How are these efforts tied to the adoption of structural practices such as implementing a new schedule, adopting a new report card, or acquiring technology? What connection is leveraged between this focus and the identification and deployment of instructional strategies and practices?
- To what extent do we find ourselves waiting to address or even ignoring strategic opportunities or learning needs because we fear lack of student commitment and capacity to achieve success? What time, effort, and energy are currently being used to develop teachers' understanding and capacity to leverage the role of learners as a key improvement strategy?
- To what extent are teachers focused on helping students see themselves and their roles as learners as being key to improving their learning experiences and results?
- To what extent do we expect that changes in conceptions, by both staff and learners, of the role students can play in learning will result in a better experience for students or increased learning? How will we monitor the results in terms of the impact of the change on students?
- What is the relationship between the cost of changing our and students' conceptions of their role in learning—in terms of dollars, time, political chips, and other factors—and anticipated results? How does this cost-benefit relationship compare to other potential change initiatives (such as smaller class sizes, changed schedules, or increased technology)?

Self from the Students' Perspective

- How will changing the role of self change students' learning experiences?
- What connections will students make between the changes in how they see themselves as learners and their school experience?
- How might students complete this prompt if changes in how educators see them and how they see themselves as learners are implemented effectively? *Before this change, we used to* _____, *but now we* _____.

Look at the tables in Appendix D related to status quo, transactional change, and transformational change and examine the questions associated with self. What types of questions do you typically hear in your school or district when you and your colleagues discuss conceptions of self? What types of questions do you typically ask? How might you change the questions you ask to find better answers and achieve better results?

Pulling the Right Levers: Lessons from the Kitchen, Campfires, Penguins, and a Bicycle

David Livingston served as a principal and central office administrator for many years in Cherry Creek, Colorado. In the fall of 1991, Livingston was principal of a new school in the district called Peakview Elementary. When the central office challenged Livingston and his staff to "rethink elementary education," they embraced the opportunity. According to Livingston, "Given that inch, we took a mile." A year before the school opening, the newly formed staff placed a single question at the core of their planning: What do we want the students to be like as a result of being with us? Deciding first on the outcomes that they expected to see in their students' lives created a powerful premise to guide their efforts. In the months and years that followed, they developed curricula, programs, and ultimately structures that would best serve their students.

It didn't take long for word of their innovative approaches and associated success to spread statewide and then around the country. The requests to visit came in waves. Different visitors labeled Peakview in different ways as they gave their reasons for wanting to see the school. Livingston and his staff fielded requests to come and see the "Technology

School" (Peakview did not equip the designated computer lab space per the blueprints and instead put five computers in each classroom—quite a step for an elementary school in 1991), the "Open Space School" (they used an "open space" floor plan that allowed for maximum flexibility in student grouping), or the "Multi-aged Classroom School" (students were clustered in cross-grade-level groups rather than by individual grades).

Peakview welcomed hundreds of visitors, and Livingston and his staff did their best to explain the school's student-centered premise and the corresponding practices. From the Peakview perspective, the staff made a series of decisions about structure based on their standards for student learning, how to best implement the instructional strategies that they believed would maximize student learning, and their focus on what they wanted their students *to be like*. To Livingston's dismay, most of the visitors were focused exclusively on the structures. After a visiting administrator would say, "We want to do this, too," the visitor would inevitably ask structural, transactional questions: How did you pay for the computers in each classroom? Could you put four or six computers in a classroom instead of five? How much time does each student get on the computer? How large is each multi-age classroom? Could we still use our desks instead of tables? Many of the visitors had mistaken the means for the ends. On the one hand, the Peakview staff wanted to tell about their journey to focus on the individual needs of each student as a learner, which had started by grappling with the transformational question, What do we want our students to be like? On the other hand, they found visitors asking a very different, transactional question: How can we get our school to look like this?

Why do some schools succeed while others fail? How do schools select and prioritize efforts to improve outcomes for students? These questions are at the heart of public education policy. How school board members, governors, and congressional representatives answer these questions has a tremendous impact on the incentives created to improve schools. In a remarkable essay titled "Knowing the Right Thing to Do: School Improvement and Performance-Based Accountability," written for the National Governors Association, Harvard's Richard Elmore (2003) argues that the conventional wisdom that guides power brokers is incorrect in that it assumes that schools fail because policy hasn't required teachers and principals to use their resources effectively, or because "the people in them lack the appropriate urgency and focus on the essential tasks of learning," or students and teachers lack "clear guidance coupled with clear rewards and sanctions" to clarify their work, or they lack the threat of closure to do what is required to succeed (p. 9).

These incorrect assumptions result in policies and external mandates that attempt to use rewards and punishments to motivate students, teachers, and principals to improve. According to Elmore, these behaviorist approaches have only a limited effect on improving outcomes because they assume that the core problem is that teachers and principals aren't working hard. In Elmore's experience—and in ours as well—teachers and principals are working extremely hard. The limited effectiveness of this approach lies in the fact that it ignores the greatest challenge faced by educational stakeholders. As Elmore states, "Knowing the right thing to do is the central problem of school improvement" (2003, p. 9).

Unfortunately, we find much of the reform agenda that schools are working on is driven by external mandates. This reality too often can result in an approach to change in schools that serves a transactional, structural question: *What does our school have to look like to be in compliance?* As illustrated in the Peakview Elementary example, this approach to improving student learning ignores a more powerful, transformational question: *What do we want our students to be like?* Regardless of the policy mandate, school leaders can choose to frame, approach, and ultimately implement those mandates in dramatically different ways. Is teacher evaluation about a transactional process designed to train principals to check boxes, dole out rewards and punishments, and fill out forms? Or is teacher evaluation a transformational opportunity to develop teachers' and principals' understanding of a shared model of effective practice as the initial step in creating systems of support that honor adults as learners on a path toward expertise in influencing student learning? Is Response to Intervention seen as a transactional sampling problem to determine which kid gets shuffled off to which classroom? Or is Response to Intervention a transformational opportunity to prioritize standards, use assessment to inform more effective teaching strategies, and empower students to develop a better understanding of themselves as learners? Regardless of the task to be accomplished, we have much influence on which levers that we choose to apply to make the work possible.

Schools that frame the work around the most powerful levers are remarkably effective in improving student learning *and* avoiding initiative fatigue. When external mandates are presented to these schools or new initiatives emerge from within, their faculty see them not as "another thing to do" but as an opportunity that can be addressed by leveraging the key work on standards, strategy, and self that underlies all of the work they do. They start with this question: *What components of this work are potentially transformational to improve student learning, and what transactional components related to structure and compliance can support the work?* The five levers can provide a powerful framework to untangle this important question and to begin to prioritize and act accordingly.

Figure 6.1 shows the five levers' relative capacity to influence change in student learning, from the relatively low-level capacity of structure at one end, to the relatively high-level capacity of self at the other. It also shows which individuals—legislators, administrators, board members, teachers, and students—are likely to play key roles in the efforts to leverage change through each of the five levers. At one end of the spectrum, legislators,

Figure 6.1 | The Five Levers' Capacity for Influencing Change and the Key Individuals Involved

Capacity for Influencing Change in Student Learning

Low Leverage → High Leverage

Structure	Sample	Standards	Strategy	Self
Logistical components of districts, schools, and classrooms, such as schedules, staffing, and administrative processes	Grouping of students in any classroom or program at any given time	Expectations for quality and articulated pathways for growth as related to student learning	The practices teachers use to help students deepen their understanding of content and improve their ability to use important skills	Beliefs that teachers and students have about their capacity to be effective

Key Individuals Involved

← Legislators/Administrators/Board Members   Teachers/Students →

administrators, and board members may be highly involved in decisions related to structure, whereas at the other end, teachers and students are central to leveraging the power of self.

Connecting Leadership and Management

A common distinction made between leadership and management is that leadership is focused on *doing the right things*, whereas management is about *doing things right*. In this context we are not speaking of formal roles and titles. Rather, we are describing the actions and activities necessary to achieve a desired outcome. This seemingly simple differentiation has significant implications for organizations, the levers they pull, and the magnitude of change they achieve, and it is especially critical during times of change. (See Figure 6.2 for a summary of the magnitude of change that one can expect for each of the five levers.)

Simply put, leadership focuses on the identification of desired outcomes, which levers to employ, and in which sequences to employ them. Leadership focuses on approaches and efforts that will have a transformative impact on student learning.

Management, on the other hand, is well suited for maintaining the status quo or engaging in transactional implementation of any of the five levers. Once desired outcomes have been established and decisions have been made regarding the appropriate levers, the process must be managed. We need to implement changes in alignment with intended outcomes, a management function. However, a management approach without the guidance and insight of leadership rarely has an impact or brings about positive changes in student learning.

Obviously, a symbiotic relationship exists between leadership and management roles and functions. Neither can be successful for long without the work and support of the other.

Metaphors to Guide Practice

At the core of the work of leadership and management is understanding both the magnitude of the change that is sought and the areas of the organization where effort should be put forth to leverage the desired results. We believe this balance occurs most effectively in organizations that engage four metaphors to guide their practice around the five levers.

Figure 6.2 | Expectations for Magnitude of Change, and Associated Results, for the Five Levers

Lever and Expected Results	Status Quo	Transactional Change	Transformational Change
Structure	Maintain existing practice	Structure changes, but learning experiences remain the same.	Structure changes and may create conditions for more effective learning, but cannot transform student learning.
Sample	Maintain existing practice	Sample changes, but learning experiences remain the same.	Sample changes and may create conditions for more effective learning, but cannot transform student learning.
Standard	Maintain existing practice	Standard changes, but learning experiences remain the same.	Standards change but will only transform student learning if new, more effective strategies are used to link students' conceptions of selves as learners to those standards.
Strategy	Maintain existing practice	Strategy is deployed but is not responsive to students' learning needs.	Strategies change but will only transform learning if they more effectively link standards to students' conceptions of themselves as learners.
Self	Maintain existing practice	New beliefs are articulated but not acted upon. Student experience remains the same.	Transformation occurs when students see themselves differently as learners as a result of the use of strategies that improve their capacity, and autonomy, to achieve or transcend standards.
Results	Identical results	New processes and procedures yield similar results.	New levels of achievement are reached; teachers and learners see themselves as more effective than they thought possible.

Metaphor 1: The Kitchen Connection—Linking Efforts and Results

The metaphor of remodeling a kitchen and expecting better-tasting food has been revisited several times through our discussions. Interestingly, if three questions had been asked prior to investing the time, effort, and resources to remodel the kitchen, the outcome might have been very different and far less disappointing.

1. What outcome are we trying to accomplish?
2. What changes will have the most direct effect on achievement of this outcome?
3. Does this change require a transactional approach (remodeling) or a transformational approach (changing cooking approaches and strategies, ingredients, and related processes)?

If the outcome the family sought most was improvement in the taste of the food, a very different set of strategies might have been employed. Furthermore, each step in the process could have been considered and decided in light of its potential to achieve the outcome sought.

We can apply similar thinking and parallel questions to our efforts to improve the level and quality of learning for students. In this context, the three questions might be these:

1. What is the outcome we are trying to influence?
2. What levers will have the most direct influence on that outcome for students?
3. Does the change require a transactional change in process or a transformational change in thought and practice?

Armed with the answers to these questions, we will be in a much better position to decide which levers hold the greatest promise to achieve the results we desire. We can also understand the order in which we might employ the levers to create the most synergy and achieve the greatest sustainability in results. If the outcome we seek is having students complete their academic day in time to mesh with bus transportation schedules, a transactional process (adjusting the structure of the daily schedule) will allow us to achieve the outcome.

However, if building student ownership of their learning (a transformational process) is the outcome we seek, we will be more successful employing levers related to helping learners see the purpose and benefits of what they are learning. We will need to leverage concepts of self and instructional strategies that give learners more voice and choice in their learning. If we find that accomplishing this outcome means that we need to use time differently, we can adjust the structure of the schedule, but we would only do so when we have employed the first two levers and discover the need to make the adjustment.

Metaphor 2: Spend Less Time Chopping Down Trees and More Time Starting Campfires

What changes, and what stays the same? This question has driven hundreds of years of scientific inquiry and invention. When two objects come in contact with one another, the results can range from the innocuous to the incredible. Pour water on a campfire, and it stops burning. Pour gasoline on a campfire, and it explodes. When two elements come in contact with each other, the interaction can be categorized as physical or chemical. In a physical interaction, particles of the substance are rearranged. No new substance is created; the substance merely takes on a different appearance.

If you've ever chopped down a tree, you've been the catalyst for a physical interaction. You've searched through the forest to find the right tree and filed the proper permits to ensure that particular tree can be removed. You've strategized by selecting a specific spot to strike repeatedly and determined a space where the tree can safely fall. You put forth a lot of time and effort to create a larger and larger cut in the trunk of the tree. Eventually, the tree falls. Make no mistake, when the tree hits the ground, it is still a tree. You continue to chop the wood. After even more effort, you've now chopped the tree into dozens of logs. For all of the energy you've transferred to the tree, you've merely rearranged its position. The organic matter that *is* that tree still exists exactly as it had moments earlier. Chopping down trees and moving logs is a metaphor for the management processes associated with maintaining the status quo and transactional change. Everyone has worked hard to rearrange the structural components, but nothing of substance has changed. You have, however, created the conditions for something transformational to occur.

In a chemical interaction, elements interact in a manner that results in something entirely different. You arrange some kindling and stack the wood into a fire pit. Unfortunately you don't have a match, so you find some materials to rub together and eventually generate enough heat to start a few small smoldering embers. Several minutes later, a small flame emerges, then a larger flame. Eventually you begin to reap the rewards of something entirely different from the solid object that stood in front of you hours earlier. The interaction among the elements has transformed the solid object into heat and light. The organic matter is different than it had been moments earlier. You are no longer the only one exerting energy; new energy is released. The logs will never return to their original state.

The most effective school leaders understand that their role is not merely to create the structures for school; their role is to ensure transformational interactions among the most critical components for learning. What changes, and what stays the same? In the same manner that this question guides scientific inquiry and innovation, we believe it should guide inquiry and innovation in schools as well. A school that engages in a significant effort to implement a *structural* change may merely be engaging in a physical interaction; *the parts are rearranged, but no new substance emerges.* The matter that *matters* in schooling has been left untouched. The *standards* for what students will learn and what will be deemed to be of quality have stayed the same. The *strategies* used to guide all students to learn those standards have stayed the same. What students and teachers believe to be true about *themselves* as learners has stayed the same. Not surprisingly, the school may look different but yield similar results for student learning.

The interaction that unleashes a *change* in matter only occurs when standards, strategies, and conceptualizations of self are used as the catalysts. When leading change in classrooms, schools, and districts, it is essential that we ask the following question to guide our planning and evaluation: What will change, and what will stay the same? Other questions follow. Are we setting out to change the school or to change experiences that most directly have an effect on student learning? Will we change the sample but use the same strategies in those classrooms? Will it be more efficient to change the strategies and leave the sample as it is? Will we restructure the elements of the school but fail to create new learning for kids?

If people in your school are tired from engaging in significant effort but experiencing little meaningful change, be sure you are not spending so much energy cutting down trees that you never get around to lighting a fire. Transformational change takes time and requires teachers and students to interact in high-leverage ways.

Metaphor 3: Think, and Act, Like a Penguin

Despite months with no daylight and temperatures that reach more than 50 degrees below zero Fahrenheit, penguins thrive in Earth's most inhospitable climate. Consider the task of obtaining food. Nothing grows on ice. From the perspective above the surface of the water, the prospect of survival seems bleak. The visible environment reveals nothing that could possibly help a species survive. If penguins are to survive, they must swim deep beneath the water's surface, often near an iceberg, to find food. They understand that although they spend most of their time above the water, they must dive deep beneath the surface to access the resources that will sustain them. Imagine the contrast of these two worlds for the penguins. Once beneath the surface, they see the abundance that is critically important for their survival; they see that the portion of the iceberg that sits above the water is only a small fraction of the total mass of the iceberg. Although they spend most of their time on the visible portion, the stability of the iceberg and their opportunity for sustenance are determined by what lies beneath the waterline.

The penguins offer a number of analogies that can be useful to framing our thinking about school improvement and the five levers. Practices associated with school structure and sample sit above the waterline and are easy for everyone to see. Whether we're talking about class size, school size, scheduling, seat time, ability grouping, or placement processes, these components are noticed by even the untrained eye. However, as we have shown, by themselves they don't improve learning. Like the icebergs, these components rest on a less visible but ultimately far more important set of practices that are out of view for almost everyone but students and teachers. Beneath the surface are the knowledge, skills, and dispositions associated with how standards will be used in those classrooms, how strategies will be deployed in a manner that best responds to student learning needs, and how conceptualizations of self will determine the extent that students are engaged in and committed to—or disenfranchised from—their learning experience. Penguins thrive on an instinct that acknowledges that what is easily seen is *not* necessarily what matters most.

Taking the idea of thinking like a penguin and applying it to the five levers can help us understand why a board member might panic after receiving several phone calls from parents because decisions about school structure have resulted in a large class in a 3rd grade classroom, yet no one seems to be aware of the amazing, learning-generating work that the teacher in that classroom is accomplishing by using formative assessments as a basis for quality feedback and instructional strategy adjustment. Meanwhile, a teacher in a small class a few doors down is offering no developmental feedback to students, is not providing students the opportunity to learn key standards, and consistently sends implicit messages to students that some of them are smart while others are not; yet the practices in this classroom do not generate a single phone call.

We've seen numerous schools and districts implement standards-based report cards but fail to build a standards-based learning system to support that tool. Confusion and frustration result. Schools that have successfully implemented standards-based report cards understand that the report card is merely the visible surface of the iceberg. A standards-based report card can be sustained only if it rests on a foundation of a standards-based system that has prioritized key standards, creates a clear distinction between criterion- and norm-referenced thinking, helps establish a shared vision of quality among teachers and students both within and across grade levels, values understanding and mastery rather than the accumulation of points, and, most important, helps students to build commitment to and take ownership for their learning. The report card is a transactional tool that fits neatly into the structure of communicating a formal record of student achievement a few times a year. The standards-based system has the potential to transform student learning because it starts with standards as the premise to guide the work done in classrooms, informs the formative strategies teachers use daily, and empowers students' conceptions of themselves as active agents in the learning process.

Figure 6.3 illustrates the penguin analogy by showing the relationship among the five levers. Structure and sample lie above the metaphorical waterline, whereas standards, strategy, and conceptions of self appear below the water line but offer the important long-term benefits of stability and sustainability.

Metaphor 4: Building Momentum to Improve Student Learning Is Like Riding a Bicycle

An interview on YouTube that has gone viral recently features a man who recalls reading, as a child, an article in *Scientific American* that changed the trajectory of his life. The article reported on a ranking of the efficiency

Figure 6.3 | The Penguin Analogy

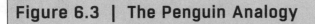

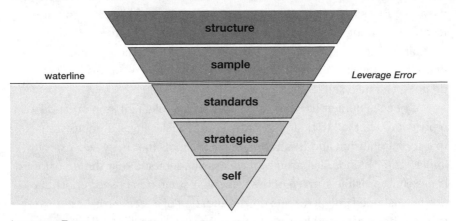

Leverage Error

The leverage error most often associated with *structure* and *sample* is the assumption that prioritizing around changes in those areas will result in an improved learning experience for students. The leverage error most often associated with *standards, strategies, and conceptualization of self* is the assumption that a transactional change in those areas will result in a transformation in teacher capacity and a transformation in student learning.

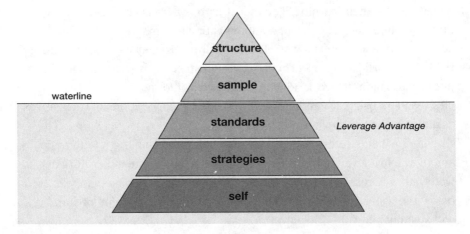

Leverage Advantage

The leverage advantage of *structure* and *sample* can only be accessed by acknowledging that those levers are merely associated with conditions for learning; they rest on a less visible, but critically important foundation. The leverage advantage of structure and sample is engaged most effectively in a context that prioritizes to ensure *strategies are more effectively utilized to connect students, and their conceptions of themselves as learners, to standards*. While these components are less visible, they are the basis for stability and sustainability of a system designed to improve learning.

of locomotion among animals. Using a formula related to weight, speed, and energy required to move a specific distance, the researchers deemed the condor as the animal kingdom's most efficient creature. Humans, he recounted, ranked somewhere in the middle of the pack. Then the researchers did something interesting. They recalculated the efficiency of humans when riding a bicycle. Immediately, humans moved to the top of the chart. This recalculation changed the way the man thought about the relationship between humans and technology. The interviewee—Steve Jobs—goes on to explain how he spent a good portion of his formative years thinking about what other efficiencies could be created through the thoughtful use of technology to transform human capacity.

We understand that riding a bicycle most efficiently requires us to use the gears we have available in appropriate and effective ways. Getting started requires engagement of the lower gears to create leverage for movement. At this level, it is fairly easy to start to pedal, but once we get moving we have a limited capacity to go very fast. As we build momentum, we shift to the higher gears to build speed and make adjustments in response to the terrain and the surfaces we encounter. We need to thoughtfully and intentionally employ the five levers we have discussed in similarly strategic ways as we approach educational change to get started effectively and build momentum and sustainability with efficiency.

When considering the five levers, think of *structure* and *sample* as the bicycle. This is the context within which the rider will experience the terrain. On its own, the bicycle creates the conditions to leverage a mechanical advantage, but without a rider the bike is useless. When the rider gets on the bike and starts to exert effort, it becomes readily apparent that the strategies the rider uses to change the bicycle's gears will determine the relationship between her effort and her results. Using the gears to maximize mechanical advantage requires the rider to understand that a direct relationship exists between the terrain, the gears, and the rider's effort. The lower gears are useful to get the rider started, but staying with those gears requires rapid pedal revolutions to simply maintain momentum. The rider can expend excessive energy without building any speed. Conversely, if a rider starts in too high a gear, she may not be able to generate enough leverage to even move the bike. Without proper support and belief in herself as a rider, she may mistakenly believe that she doesn't have the internal capacity to move the bike. However, when done effectively, the rider starts moving in the lower gear and, as she gains momentum and balance, shifts to larger gears and builds speed. The large gear that wouldn't budge just a few minutes ago now gives the rider the thrill of movement at speeds she never thought possible. As she moves forward and leverages the gears appropriately, she is able to go dramatically faster without having to exert as much effort.

The *standards* are the terrain. The efficiency of the bicycle occurs because the rider herself is instantaneously responsive to the terrain. She sees what is on the horizon and can anticipate how to most efficiently leverage next steps. She understands the relationship between the effort she puts forth and the results she gets. She has maximized the leverage advantage.

Suppose, however, that the same rider was given a different bicycle (structure and sample) but couldn't see the terrain. She couldn't anticipate the relationship between her efforts and the route, let alone the strategy to navigate the terrain most effectively. Furthermore, suppose she didn't understand the relationship between the gears and her effort. Each time she shifted the gears they moved randomly—sometimes making it harder to pedal and other times making it easier. Shifting gears while going uphill could mean the task suddenly became so difficult that her progress stopped entirely. Shifting gears while going down a slope could leave her pedaling harder but not moving any faster. In time, she might completely disconnect the relationship between her efforts and the results she obtained, leaving her with a sense that the mechanical advantage of the levers was completely out of her control and a sense that other people were just naturally good at riding bikes, but she was not.

Let's now apply the bicycle metaphor to teaching and learning. We might think of the lower gears as making changes in the instructional strategies we use and adjusting the learning roles and relationships of learners. We know we can generate increases in student learning by using strategies effectively and engaging students with their learning in ways that build efficacy, ownership, and independence. These "lower gears" create leverage or torque to increase learning outcomes.

However, in the absence of a clear focus on standards and expectations for quality, students may develop independence but may not have the opportunity to learn the essential content and skills articulated in the standards. Or, they may spend excessive time attempting to master specific standards that are better addressed at another point in the curriculum. In short, we may find ourselves having inefficiently invested our energy and the learning focus and efforts of our students. Standards here are like the terrain for the cyclist; our effort and attention must be allocated in response to the challenges and expectations we face.

Once we have effectively positioned learners for success and implemented the strategies necessary to begin to move learning forward and we have a clear understanding of and focus on the standards to be met, our interest and energy can shift to efforts to further accelerate and sustain momentum. At this point the rider may benefit from a new bike. We may find that by using time and classroom space differently, we can remove distractions and improve continuity for learners. We might discover that by grouping and regrouping students we can increase the productivity of specific instructional strategies.

If our efforts had started with changes in schedules, use of space, or regrouping of students, we likely would have discovered that those efforts alone would have been no more effective than trying to ride a new bicycle without understanding how to ride a bicycle, let alone knowing how to efficiently operate the gears. Conversely, when we start by taking advantage of the leverage or "torque" created by the lower gears of learner engagement and instructional strategy, we can later leverage structure and sample to help learners to more efficiently and consistently navigate and progress toward standards.

Reform, Invention, and Innovation in Education

Schools in the United States have been subjected to wave after wave of ideas, initiatives, programs, and sanctions aimed at making them capable of meeting society's need for well-educated citizens and skilled, motivated employees who can ensure the nation's economic competitiveness and well-being. Yet the schools' capacity appears to have changed little, for better or worse. The case is well made and documented in Charles Payne's book, *So Much Reform, So Little Change* (2008).

Might it be that we have been focusing in the wrong places and pulling the wrong levers? Given the size of the United States' financial investment in schools, especially when compared to the rest of the world, it is difficult to argue that the problem is underinvestment. On almost any measure, the

United States is among the highest spenders when it comes to education. Yet the results do not reflect commensurate academic outcomes among our youth (OECD, 2010).

Meanwhile, educators are working harder, under more difficult conditions. Outcome standards are rising with each new wave of education accountability initiatives. Rankings place American students in the middle of international comparisons, and politicians are looking to blame educators. Educator performance evaluations are increasingly tied to student test performance, regardless of the size and composition of the teaching assignment. Public-employee worker rights, wages, and benefits are under pressure, and fears are growing that they are slipping away. Concurrently, teachers are being asked to work with a student body that is more diverse than it was even a few decades ago—and that will become even more so (Perez & Hirschman, 2009). And, for the first time in U.S. history, learners are not necessarily convinced that education, the economy, and society hold the promise that their lives will be better than those of their parents.

The approach employed to improve the capacity and performance of U.S. schools for the past several decades has been to *reform*. For the most part, these efforts have been to make incremental improvements to the current system without addressing the core design of the system around *self* and *strategy*. Educators have looked for and selected, for the most part, the *standard*, *sample*, and *structure* levers with the expectation that they could lift school outcomes to acceptable levels. No Child Left Behind attempted to lift performance by gradually increasing *standards* over time while increasing the focus on the performance of subgroups of students. The effort increased awareness of the gaps between groups of learners but did little to lift the overall performance of schools and certainly did not solve the performance challenge facing the nation's schools. Meanwhile, other nations, such as Finland and Singapore, made strategic investments in the connection between the learner and learning and the instructional strategies and approaches educators employed with learners. The result has been a widening gap between the performance of American schools and the educational systems that lead the world (Tucker, 2011). A growing realization has emerged that efforts to improve the system with current incremental, low-leverage initiatives are too slow, expensive, and ineffective to warrant continuing (Fullan, 2011). We can no longer afford to accept such significant leveraging errors when it comes to the education of our children.

Some might suggest we consider the more radical approach of *inventing* a whole new system or concept of teaching and learning. However, such a step risks not understanding key implications and making key decisions about the education system and about learning without the benefits of experience and research. This approach means abandoning what works in the current system in favor of the significant risks that accompany the implementation of an untried, unproven system. Certainly, we need to continue to press the limits of our knowledge and practice to find new and better ways of educating our youth, but we cannot afford to sacrifice a generation while we test and study.

Another alternative is to revisit and apply what we know about learners and learning to design a new system that has greater capacity and that can take advantage of the current education research base by applying it in new ways. This approach, *innovation*, involves examination of current system strategies, standards, sample, and structures in light of what learners need to be successful, and transforming them in ways that we know can better engage learners; build efficacy, ownership, and independence; and produce better, more robust education outcomes. In short, the innovation approach takes what we know about learners and learning as the premise to guide efforts for the transformation of schools and students' learning experiences in those schools.

This alternative suggests that we move away from the assembly-line, batch-processing approach and focus more on how best to meet the needs and tap the interests and talents of individual learners. We might abandon the rigid time schedules and calendars that confine learning and instead make learning the measuring stick to which we pay most attention. We can focus on developing competency and proficiency to measure and track learning growth rather than rely on proxy measures such as grades, credits, and grade levels. Interestingly, prioritizing around standards, strategy, and self has a solid basis in existing research (see Appendix B). However, the current educational system makes full application of the research difficult and at times impossible (Black & Wiliam, 1998; Bloom, 1984; Hattie, 2009).

We have shown how pulling the levers of *self* and *strategy* can increase the connection learners have with *standards* to guide their learning and the growth in learning performance that results. We have discussed how these three high-capacity levers are catalysts for changes that occur in the context of *sample* and *structure* to increase the impact of carefully selected and thoughtfully applied instructional practices. The potential also exists to use this framework to significantly improve the capacity and performance of the larger educational system within which we are working to maximize the learning and preparation of our youth.

We cannot change or ignore the growing pressures being placed on our schools and those who learn and work in them. But we can redesign the approach and functioning of our schools to take advantage of what we know is effective for learners and learning. We can leverage the most powerful elements in the learning environment to overcome many of the challenges we face and create opportunities and support for all learners to achieve at high levels.

The temptation to change structure as the catalyst for improvement is strong. The allure of relatively easy, tangible, politically popular, silver-bullet solutions can be difficult to resist. But changing school structure, adopting new standards, or moving kids into different sections or programs typically results in little positive effect on student learning. We argue that pulling these levers will affect student learning only when it is done in a manner that allows for the use of more effective instructional practices that allow students to interact with standards in a meaningful way and that support the individual students' sense of self-agency related to their learning.

Conclusion

We have invested countless hours and untold financial resources in attempts to make the changes and generate the learning improvements necessary to ensure that our education system can serve the needs of our economy and society, but without generating adequate results. To the extent that we have fallen short, it has not been for lack of effort, commitment, or investment.

Efforts focused on large-scale reform haven't been successful because those efforts have failed to change schools. *They haven't been successful because, too often, the transactional, structural approaches that can change schools have little or nothing to do with the less visible but far more powerful strategies required to change students' learning experiences in those schools.* We began this book with two quotes: "Give me a lever long enough and a fulcrum on which to place it, and I shall move the world" by Archimedes and "There is no world. There's only 6 billion understandings of it. And if you change one person's understanding of what they're capable of, you've changed the whole thing" by Drew Dudley. In theory, if we had a lever long enough, we could change every school. But if those efforts failed to change the point of contact that occurs between teachers and students in the classroom, our efforts will have been in vain.

We need to reprioritize our efforts in a manner that focuses on students. We believe that by prioritizing our discourse, efforts, policies, and practices around more effectively using standards to guide the use of strategies that influence learning, we can change students' understanding of what they are capable of. If we prioritize our efforts to make the change that matters, we can change the whole thing.

Appendix A: *Prioritizing Efforts to Improve Student Learning*

This table can be used to guide dialogue when working to prioritize strategic efforts, initiatives, and policies to improve student learning.

Three Critical Questions for Prioritizing Efforts to Improve Student Learning:

1. What is the student learning outcome we are trying to influence?
2. What levers will have the most direct impact on influencing that outcome for students?
3. What is the magnitude of change necessary to obtain the results we seek? Ongoing management of the status quo? Transactional change in process and procedures? Transformational change in our understanding of the work and our relationship to the work?

	Do More of This	Do Less of This
Structure	Emphasizing the *why* of changes in structure. How will the change in structure more effectively leverage standards, strategy, and conceptualizations of self?	Assuming that the implementation of structural changes will result in different learning experiences for students
Sample	If students are clustered or grouped differently, considering how standards, strategy, and conceptualizations of self can be more effectively addressed to support individual student needs	Assuming that because students are grouped differently they will have a more effective learning experience
Standards	Using standards as the premise to guide students' and teachers' efforts. When the standards change, formative and summative classroom assessments need to look different as well	Assuming that aligning standards to existing curriculum will result in changes in instruction and assessment
Strategy	Ensuring that development of teacher expertise—using the right skill at the right time to obtain the desired effect—is the top priority for supervision, goal setting, and professional development	Assuming that the same few instructional strategies can be used all the time to affect student learning
Self	Acknowledging that addressing student confidence, interest, motivation, engagement, and autonomy is central to our work as educators	Assuming that confidence, interest, motivation, engagement, and autonomy are fixed characteristics within each child and cannot be influenced by educators

Appendix B: *Using the Five Levers to Discern Patterns in Research Findings on Effective Practices*

Lezotte and Snyder's *What Effective Schools Do: Re-envisioning the Correlates* (2011)	• High expectations for success (standards) • Strong instructional leadership (strategy) • Clear and focused mission (strategy) • Opportunity to learn/time on task (strategy) • Frequent monitoring of student progress (strategy, self) • Safe and orderly environment (structure, strategy) • Positive home—school relations (strategy, self)
Marzano, Waters, and McNulty's *School Leadership That Works* (2005)	• Opportunity to learn (standards, strategy) • Adequate instructional time (standards, strategy) • Identification of essential understandings (standards) • Commitment to teach essential content (standards, strategy) • Protection of time for instruction and learning (structure, strategy)
McKinsey's *How the World's Best-Performing School Systems Come Out on Top* (2007)	• Hiring the right people to become teachers (strategy, self) • Developing teachers' capacity to be effective (strategy, self) • Ensuring the system is able to deliver the best instruction to every child (standards, strategy, self)
Sign-Posts of Excellence in Hattie's *Visible Learning* (2009)	• Teachers are among the most powerful influences (self). • Teachers need to be directive, caring, and engaged (self). • Teachers need to provide meaningful and appropriate feedback (strategy). • Teachers need to know the learning intentions and success criteria of their lessons (standards, self). • Teachers need to understand that it is not the knowledge or ideas they are teaching but, rather, the learner's construction of knowledge and ideas that is critical (standards, strategy, self). • School leaders and teachers need to create school, staff room, and classroom environments where error is welcomed and participants feel safe to learn, relearn, and explore knowledge (self, strategy).

Appendix C: *Examples of School and Classroom Components Associated with Each Lever*

Structure	Sample	Standards	Strategy	Self
• Acceleration/ retention • Access to technology • Accountability incentives/ sanctions • Age cohorts • Attendance • Block scheduling • Calendar • Class size • Compensation schedules • Credits • Daily schedule • Late starts/ early-release collaboration time • Organization of curriculum • Public/ private • Reporting (grades) • School size • Seat time • Staff development time • Staffing; teaching, support, and administrative • Supervision/ evaluation process • Testing • Uniforms • Voucher/ choice	• Ability grouping • Age cohort • Gender grouping • Geographic boundaries/ attendance zones • Gifted and talented • Magnet/ specialty programs/ schools/ cohorts • Placement processes • School choice processes or programs • Special education	• Articulated academic standards • College entrance exams • Criteria for grades and advancement • External high-stakes testing • Gateway testing • Graduation requirements (competency or credits; number and distribution) • Prerequisites • Teacher certification • Teacher expectations • Teacher quality	• Alignment among curriculum, instruction, and assessment • Classroom management strategies • Content sequencing and scaffolding • Curriculum design • Feedback • Instructional strategies • Instructionally responsive assessment practices • Professional development • Purpose, meaning, relevance, authenticity • Student self-assessment • Task design • Teacher self-assessment	• Agency • Aspirations • Beliefs about one's capacity to learn • Cultural identity • Effective effort • Engagement • Family/ community context • Gender • Learned helplessness • Learning orientation vs. performance orientation • Learning preferences (modalities) • Motivation, engagement, efficacy, ownership, independence • Past experience • Persistence/ commitment • Purpose, meaning, relevance • Relationships with peers/teacher • Self-determination • Self-efficacy • Stereotype threat • Strengths/ assets

Appendix D: *Planning Questions Related to Status Quo, Transactional Change, and Transformational Change*

Planning Questions That Indicate Efforts to Maintain the Status Quo				
Planning questions that maintain the status quo focus exclusively on the implementation of processes that perpetuate existing practices.				
Structure	Sample	Standards	Strategy	Self
• When should the process occur? • Who should do the process? • What tools or resources are necessary for the process? • Where will the process occur? • How will we know the process has been completed?	• When will we place students? • Who will communicate results of placement decisions? • What criteria will be used to decide placement? • Where will students be placed? • How will placements be communicated?	• When in the sequence should the standards be applied? • Who will communicate the standards? • Who is responsible for teaching which standards? • What criteria and processes will be used to measure compliance or proficiency? • How can we demonstrate we're currently teaching these already?	• When and how will we evaluate the teaching strategies that are used? • What process is used to decide/teach strategies? • Where will training occur? • Who will provide the training? • How will we know teachers have been trained?	• When do we orient students to existing rules and expectations? • Who is responsible for helping kids navigate the school structure? • What process will be used to inform students of their progress and status? • When will summative results about student achievement be communicated? • How will students be held accountable?
For example, suppose a school plans to maintain its current system of grading and reporting. Planning and efforts related to report cards would be around logistical components such as when grades are due, to whom they are submitted, how they will be submitted, and who will distribute them, among others.				

Planning Questions That Indicate Efforts to Make Transactional Change

Planning questions related to transactional change seek changes in current practices but do not change underlying assumptions about teaching and learning; they typically require different logistical approaches but do not require new or different ways of thinking about leveraging student learning.

Structure	Sample	Standards	Strategy	Self
• When will we deploy the new structure? • Who will be involved in the decision-making process? The implementation process? • What resources or training are required? • Where will the structure be deployed? • How will we communicate the change? • How will we know the implementation was successful?	• When will we deploy new groupings or the criteria for grouping? • Who will be placed where? • Who will determine placements? • What are the revised criteria for placements? • Where will students go or report? • How will we communicate the change in groupings or placements?	• When should students be held accountable for which standards? • Who is responsible for teaching the revised standards? • What are the new standards? • Where should the standards be taught? • How should curriculum be modified to ensure standards are addressed?	• When will we teach the strategies we want teachers to use? • Who decides the strategies? • What process is used to decide/teach strategies? • Where will training occur? • Who will provide the training? • How will we know teachers have been trained?	• When will students engage in activities that help adults understand who the students are as learners? • Who will administer assessments/tools to create a learner profile? • What instruments, and/or strategies, processes are used to develop learner profiles? • Where in the grade progression will learner profiles be developed? How will they be used?

For example, a school is moving from an antiquated paper-and-pencil report card to an online report card system. The shift in practice has nothing to do with the content of the report card; the shift in practice simply requires a different process for how grades are entered and how they can be accessed. This change could also include a change in cut scores, such as a shift from a 90% to a 93% for an *A*, or a change in descriptors from an *A* through *F* system to an Advanced through Minimal system. Conversations and planning would be associated with the new ways of calculating grades and the new methods used to enter and upload grades in the electronic system.

Planning Questions That Indicate Efforts to Engage in Transformational Change				
Planning questions related to transformational change challenge the underlying assumptions about the relationship among school structure and student and adult beliefs about learning, yielding a more effective learning experience for students.				
Structure	Sample	Standards	Strategy	Self
• When will we be in a position to ensure that changes in structure will result in a different and more effective learning experience for students? • Who will notice that the change has occurred in a manner that increases student capacity to learn? • Whose learning will benefit from the change? Whose will be inhibited by the change? In what ways? • What elements of structure need to be changed to allow strategies to have the intended impact on student learning or student experience?	• When will we be in a position to ensure that changes in the sample will result in a different and more effective learning experience for students? • Whose learning needs are served by the existing sampling? Whose needs are not served? • What are the intended and unintended consequences of current sampling procedures? Proposed procedures? • Where are students served in a manner that best aligns their learning needs with where they spend the majority of their school time?	• When should particular standards be emphasized to inform the teacher's effort for instruction and feedback to students? • When should students prioritize effort toward which standards? • What standards are more important than others? • Where can prioritized standards be implemented and integrated across the curriculum?	• What strategies can educators use to best leverage student learning? • What strategies can students use to best leverage their own learning?	• When will students engage in activities that help them understand themselves as a learner? • Who will engage students in processes that develop their effective strategies that result in greater learner capacity? • What feedback loops and support systems will assist students and teachers in supporting one another's learning? • Where will students be engaged with adults in developing their learning path?

Planning Questions That Indicate Efforts to Engage in Transformational Change				
Planning questions related to transformational change challenge the underlying assumptions about the relationship among school structure and student and adult beliefs about learning, yielding a more effective learning experience for students.				
Structure	Sample	Standards	Strategy	Self
• Where will there be an impact on student capacity to learn? • How does changing the structure influence the students' experience in ways that are likely to generate more learning? • How does the current structure impede student learning? • How does the current structure prevent the implementation of intended strategies? • How will we know the impact of the change on student learning? On student conceptions of self?	• How does changing the sample yield access to more effective opportunities for learning?	• How will the standards be implemented in a manner that allows students to describe their current performance, the desired performance, and the effort necessary to close the gap between the two?		• How will the feedback loops and support systems develop authentic engagement, accountability, and ownership for the student?
For example, a school is trying to reconceptualize grading from a token-economy approach of completing tasks and accumulating points to a standards-based system in which students are empowered to monitor their progress and adjust their efforts to achieve specific learning goals. Here the shift is not about a report card or reporting tools but about teachers using assessment differently and students seeing themselves differently as a result of a reconceptualization of the interrelationship among standards, strategy, and self. Conversations and planning for transformational change require discussions around the fundamental, often unspoken assumptions related to why we give grades in the first place.				

Appendix E: *Three Critical Planning Questions and Sample Scenarios*

These scenarios demonstrate how leveraging structure and sample can result in dramatically different outcomes for students than leveraging standards and strategies.

Three Critical Questions for Prioritizing Efforts to Improve Student Learning:

   1. What is the student outcome we are trying to influence?
   2. What levers will have the most direct impact on influencing that outcome for students?
   3. Does the change require a transactional change in process or a transformational change in thought and practice?

Through the Five-Lever Framework, it is critically important to be specific about the change that is sought. Typically, a school seeks changes to improve student knowledge or skills. To best understand what students need to improve their knowledge or skills, the change should be viewed through the eyes of the student.

Suppose a school is implementing practices related to Response to Intervention. Consider the following scenarios. In Scenario 1, the structures related to Response to Intervention are seen as the means and the ends to the implementation. Structural components are leveraged through a change in the daily schedule, and sampling is leveraged through targeted intervention groups.

Scenario 1: Transactional Approach Leveraging Structure and Sample		
	Students Used to...	Now They...
Structure	... have to stay after school for additional assistance.	... have a resource period to access additional assistance.
Sample	... be placed in intervention groups.	(Same as before)
Standards	... take benchmark assessments to identify their deficits.	(Same as before)
Strategy	... receive similar instructional strategies in whole-group instruction.	(Same as before)

Scenario 1: Transactional Approach Leveraging Structure and Sample		
	Students Used to...	Now They...
Self	[It was assumed that students]... believe they can complete the skill if they just apply themselves.	(Same as before)
Resulting in...	Status quo	Change in school structure, but little change in learning experience, resulting in similar levels of learning.

In Scenario 1, structure and sample have been leveraged. However, it is unlikely that these changes will have any direct impact on student learning. The structure for delivery of the targeted intervention was changed, but at the point of contact between the teacher and student, the students' learning experiences have remained largely the same.

Now consider Scenario 2.

Scenario 2: Transformational Approach Leveraging Standards, Strategy, and Self		
	Students Used to...	Now They...
Structure	... have to stay after school for additional assistance.	... access targeted intervention throughout the school day.
Sample	... be placed in intervention groups.	... stay in heterogeneous groups.
Standards	... take benchmark assessments to identify their deficits.	... take benchmark assessments clearly linked to the progression of learning targets. Targets are articulated in a manner that students can explain.
Strategy	... receive similar instructional strategies in whole-group instruction.	... have prioritized learning targets, student- and teacher-identified goals, and strategies aligned by teacher to instructional need. The goal is to teach skill and develop student autonomy in using the targeted strategy.
Self	[It was assumed that students]... believe they can complete the skill if they just apply themselves.	[It is assumed that students]... need affirmation that effort will result in improved learning and may be saddled by the belief that their current inability to demonstrate knowledge or skill is evidence of an inability to do so in the future.

	Students Used to...	Now They...
Scenario 2: Transformational Approach Leveraging Standards, Strategy, and Self		
Resulting in...	Status quo	... experience an emphasis on change in students' and teacher's ability to link strategies to standards, resulting in a different learning experience for students.

Appendix F: *Five-Lever Planning Template*

Five-Lever Planning Template

1. What is the student outcome we are trying to influence?

Current State: Currently, students...	*Desired State:* In the future, they will...

2. What levers will have the most direct impact on influencing that outcome? (Rank-order 1 through 5)

	Structure—Changing the schedule, amount of class time, etc.
	Sample—Grouping students differently than currently
	Standards—Clarifying expectations for student learning
	Strategy—Using different instructional strategies that are better aligned to student learning needs/student strengths
	Self—Developing students' self-perceptions and beliefs in the relationship between effort and results

Explain your rationale for your response to Item 2:

3. Does the change require leveraging a transactional change in process or a transformational change in thought and practice?

	Transactional change in process involves student and teacher behaviors remaining largely the same, but the processes related to these behaviors are changed. For example, a new report card is implemented or a new textbook is adopted, but the processes of curriculum, instruction, and assessment remain largely the same.

Five-Lever Planning Template
	Transformational change in thought and practice involves students or teachers viewing the assumptions that underlie the nature of their work, and resultant practices, differently. For example, a new report card is implemented and requires students and teachers to change how they use formative and summative assessments to inform efforts to improve, access, and provide feedback *and* calculate grades.
Explain your rationaie for your response to Item 3:
Synthesis statement: If students are going to _____ [summarize desired state], then we will need to [summarize Items 2 and 3 above] _____.

References

Ames, C. (1992). Classrooms: Goals, structures, and student motivation. *Journal of Educational Psychology, 84*(3), 261–271. Retrieved from http://www.unco.edu/cebs/psychology/kevinpugh/motivation_project/resources/ames92.pdf

Ames, C., & Archer, J. (1988). Achievement goals in the classroom: Students' learning strategies and motivation processes. *Journal of Educational Psychology, 80*(3), 260–267.

Bandura, A. (1986). *Social foundations of thought and action: A social cognitive theory.* Englewood Cliffs, NJ: Prentice Hall.

Bandura, A. (1991, February). Human agency: The rhetoric and the reality. *American Psychologist, 46*(2), 157–162. doi:10.1037/0003-066X.46.2.157

Barber, M., & M. Mourshed. (2007). *How the world's best-performing school systems come out on top.* Retrieved from http://mckinseyonsociety.com/downloads/reports/Education/Worlds_School_Systems_Final.pdf

Barth, R. S. (1997, March 5). The leader as learner. *Education Week, 16*(23), 56.

Bass, B. M. (1985). *Leadership and performance beyond expectations.* New York: Free Press.

Bifulco, R., & Ladd, H. F. (2006). The impacts of charter schools on student achievement: Evidence from North Carolina. *Education Finance and Policy, 1*(1), 50–90. doi:10.1162/edfp.2006.1.1.50

Black, P., & Wiliam, D. (1998). Assessment and classroom learning. *Assessment in Education: Principles, Policy and Practice, 5*(1), 7–73.

Bloom, B. S. (1984). The 2 sigma problem: The search for methods of group instruction as effective as one-to-one tutoring. *Educational Researcher, 13*(6), 4–16.

Brewster, C., & Fager, J. (2000, October). *Increasing student engagement and motivation: From time-on-task to homework.* Portland, OR: Northwest Regional Educational Laboratory. Retrieved from http://home.comcast. net/~reasoned/4410/CRM%20Concept%20Map%20with%20Links/html-tdm-model-hyperlinke_files/motivationforstudents_13.pdf

Britton, E., Paine, L., Pimm, D., & Raizen, S. (2003). *Comprehensive teacher induction: Systems for early career learning.* Dordrecht, the Netherlands: Kluwer Academic Publishers.

Brookhart, S. (2013). *How to create and use rubrics for formative assessment and grading.* Alexandria, VA: ASCD.

Brown, J. (2004). Grade-A perfect. *Principal Leadership, 5*(2), 28–32. Retrieved from http://www.principals.org/portals/0/content/48603.pdf

Burns, J. M. (1978). *Leadership.* New York: Harper & Row.

Butler, D. L., & Winne, P. H. (1995). Feedback and self-regulated learning: A theoretical synthesis. *Review of Educational Research, 65*(3), 245–281. doi: 10.3102/00346543065003245

Carr, J.F. & Harris, D.E. (2001). *Succeeding with standards: Linking curriculum, assessment, and action planning.* Alexandria, VA: ASCD.

Center for American Progress. (2010, April 22). Expanded learning time by the numbers: The traditional school calendar is failing to meet many students' needs. Retrieved from http://www.americanprogress.org/issues/education/news/2010/04/22/7716/expanded-learning-time-by-the-numbers

Center for Research on Education Outcomes (CREDO). (2009). *Multiple choice: Charter school performance in 16 states.* Stanford, CA: Stanford University.

Cherepinsky, V. (2011). Self-reflective grading: Getting students to learn from their mistakes. *PRIMUS: Journal of Problems, Resources, and Issues in Mathematics Undergraduate Studies, 21*(3), 294–301.

Clarke, D., & Clarke, B. A. (2008, Autumn). Is time up for ability grouping? *EQ Australia,* 31–33.

Cocking, R. R., & Bransford, J. (Eds.). (2000). *How people learn: Brain, mind, experience, and school.* Washington, DC: National Academies Press.

Cosden, M., Zimmer, J., & Tuss, P. (1993). The impact of age, sex, and ethnicity on kindergarten entry and retention decisions. *Educational Evaluation and Policy Analysis, 15*(2), 209–222.

Crooks, T. J. (1988). The impact of classroom evaluation practices on students. *Review of Educational Research, 58*(4), 438–481. doi:10.2307/1170281

Csikszentmihalyi, M. (2004, February). *Flow, the secret to happiness.* TED Talks. [Video]. Retrieved from http://www.ted.com/talks/mihaly_csikszentmihalyi_on_flow.html

Cunningham, P. M., & Allington, R. L. (2010). *Classrooms that work: They can all read and write.* New York: Pearson.

Danielson, C. (2007). *Enhancing professional practice: A framework for teaching.* Alexandria, VA: ASCD.

David, J. L. (2008, March). What research says about… grade retention. *Educational Leadership, 65*(6), 83–84.

Davidovich, R., Nikolay, P., Laugerman, & Commodore, C. (2010). *Beyond school improvement: The journey to innovative leadership.* Thousand Oaks, CA: Corwin.

Deci, E. L., & Ryan, R. M. (2000). The "what" and "why" of goal pursuits: Human needs and the self-determination of behavior. *Psychological Inquiry, 11*(4), 227–268.

Donovan, M. S., & Bransford, J. D. (Eds.). (2005). *How students learn: History, mathematics, and science in the classroom.* Washington, DC: National Academies Press.

Dornbusch, S. M. (1994, February). *Off the track.* Presidential address at the biennial meeting of the Society for Research on Adolescence, San Diego, CA.

Dweck, C. S. (2000). *Self-theories: Their role in motivation, personality, and development.* Philadelphia: Psychology Press.

Dweck, C. S. (2006). *Mindset: The new psychology of success.* New York: Random House.

Dweck, C. S. (2007). The perils and promises of praise. *Educational Leadership, 65*(2), 34–39.

Dweck, C. S. (2010). Mind-sets and equitable education. *Principal Leadership, 10*(5), 26–29.

Dweck, C. S., & Elliott, E. S. (1983). Achievement motivation. In P. Mussen & E. M. Hetherington (Eds.), *Handbook of child psychology.* New York: Wiley.

Elmore, (2003). *Knowing the right thing to do: School improvement and performance-based accountability.* Washington, DC: National Governors Association. Available: http://www.nga.org/files/live/sites/NGA/files/pdf/0803KNOWING.pdf

Ericsson, K. A. (2006). The influence of experience and deliberate practice on the development of superior expert performance. In K. A. Ericsson, N. Charness, P. Feltovich, & R. R. Hoffman (Eds.), *Cambridge handbook of expertise and expert performance* (pp. 685–706). Cambridge, UK: Cambridge University Press.

Ericsson, K. A., Krampe, R. T., & Tesch-Romer, C. (1993). The role of deliberate practice in the acquisition of expert performance. *Psychological Review, 100*(3), 363–406.

Farkas, S., Duffett, A., & Loveless, T. (2008). *High-achieving students in the era of No Child Left Behind.* Washington, DC: Thomas B. Fordham Institute.

Fehr, S. (2001). *The role of the educational supervisor in United States public schools from 1970 to 2000 as reflected in the supervision literature.* (Unpublished doctoral dissertation). Pennsylvania State University.

Fullan, M. (2001). *Leading in a culture of change*. San Francisco: Jossey-Bass.

Fullan, M. (2011, May). *Choosing the wrong drivers for whole system reform*. (Centre for Strategic Education Seminar Series Paper No. 204). Available: www.michaelfullan.ca/home_articles/SeminarPaper204.pdf.

Gardner, H. (1991). *The unschooled mind: How children think and how schools should teach*. New York: Basic Books.

Gawande, A. (2007). *Better: A surgeon's notes on performance*. New York: Metropolitan Books.

Gladwell, M. (2008). *Outliers: The story of success*. New York: Little, Brown.

Grant, H., & Dweck, C. S. (2003). Clarifying achievement goals and their impact. *Journal of Personality and Social Psychology, 85*(3), 541–553. doi:10.1037/0022-3514.85.3.541

Guskey, T. R. (2011, November). Five obstacles to grading reform. *Educational Leadership, 69*(3), 16–21.

Guskey, T. R., & Jung, L. A. (2013). *Answers to essential questions about standards, assessments, grading, and reporting*. Thousand Oaks, CA: Corwin Press.

Hall, G., & Hord, S. (2010). *Implementing change: Patterns, principles, and potholes* (3rd ed.). Upper Saddle River, NJ: Prentice Hall.

Halpern, D. F., Eliot, L., Bigler, R. S., Fabes, R. A., Hanish, L. D., Hyde, J., Liben, L. S., & Martin, C. L. (2011, September 23). The pseudoscience of single-sex schooling. *Science, 333*(6050), 1706–1707.

Hamre, B., & Pianta, R. (2001). Early teacher–child relationships and the trajectory of children's school outcomes through eighth grade. *Child Development, 72*, 625–638.

Hattie, J. (2009). *Visible learning: A synthesis of over 800 meta-analyses relating to achievement*. London: Routledge.

Hattie, J. (2011). *Visible learning for teachers: Maximizing impact on learning*. London: Routledge.

Haycock, K. (1998). Good teaching matters… a lot. *Thinking K–16, 3*(2), 1–14.

Heifetz, R. A., & Linsky, M. (2002). *Leadership on the line: Staying alive through the dangers of leading*. Boston: Harvard Business School Press.

Hipp, K. K., & Huffman, J. B. (Eds.). (2010). *Demystifying professional learning communities: School leadership at its best*. Lanham, MD: Rowman & Littlefield Education.

Holthouse, D. (2010, Spring). Gender education: Separate but effective? *Teaching Tolerance, 46*(37). Available: http://www.tolerance.org/magazine/number-37-spring-2010/feature/gender-segregation-separate-effective

Howard, J. (1990). *Getting smart: The social construction of intelligence*. Lexington, MA: Efficacy Institute.

Howard, J. (1995). You can't get there from here: The need for a new logic in education reform. *Daedalus, 124*(4), 85–92.

Hunter, M. (1985). What's wrong with Madeline Hunter? *Educational Leadership*, *42*(5), 57–60.

Hunter, M., & Russell, D. (2006). Planning for effective instruction: Lesson design. In B. A. Marlowe & A. S. Canestrari (Eds.), *Educational psychology in context: Readings for future teachers* (pp. 4–12). Thousand Oaks, CA: Sage.

Johnston, P. H. (2004). *Choice words: How our language affects children's learning.* Portland, ME: Stenhouse.

Kahneman, D. (2011). *Thinking fast and slow.* New York: Farrar, Straus & Giroux.

Kaplan, A., Gheen, M., & Midgley, C. (2002). Classroom goal structure and student disruptive behaviour. *British Journal of Educational Psychology, 72*(6), 191–211.

Keene, E. O., & Zimmerman, S. (2007). *Mosaic of thought: The power of comprehension strategy instruction* (2nd ed.). Portsmouth, NH: Heinemann.

Keller, J. (2000, February). *How to integrate learner motivation planning into lesson planning: The ARCS model approach.* Paper presented at VII Semanario, Santiago, Cuba. Retrieved from http://mailer.fsu.edu/~jkeller/Articles/Keller%202000%20ARCS%20Lesson%20Planning.pdf

Kirp, D. (2013, February 9). The secret to fixing bad schools. *New York Times.* Available: http://www.nytimes.com/2013/02/10/opinion/sunday/the-secret-to-fixing-bad-schools.html?pagewanted=all&_r=0

Knight, J. (2011). *Unmistakable impact: A partnership approach for dramatically improving instruction.* Thousand Oaks, CA: Corwin Press.

Kohn, A. (1993, September). Choices for children: Why and how to let students decide. *Phi Delta Kappan.* Retrieved from http://www.alfiekohn.org/teaching/cfc.htm

Kohn, A. (1995, April 19). Newt Gingrich's reading plan. *Education Week.* Retrieved from http://www.alfiekohn.org/teaching/edweek/ngrp.htm

Kohn, A. (1999, March). From degrading to de-grading. *High School Magazine, 6*(5), 38–43. Retrieved from http://www.alfiekohn.org/teaching/fdtd-g.htm

Kohn, A. (2010). How to create nonreaders: Reflections on motivation, learning, and sharing power. *English Journal, 100*(1). Retrieved from http://www.alfiekohn.org/teaching/nonreaders.htm

Lemov, D. (2010). *Teach like a champion: 49 techniques that put students on the path to college.* San Francisco: Jossey-Bass.

Lezotte, L. W., & Snyder, K. M. (2011). *What effective schools do: Re-envisioning the correlates.* Bloomington, IN: Solution Tree Press.

Loveless, T. (2012). *How well are American students learning?* (Brown Center Report). Washington, DC: Brookings Institution.

Loveless, T. (2013). *The resurgence of ability grouping and persistence of tracking.* (Part II of the 2013 Brown Center Report on American Education). Washington, DC: Brookings Institution.

Lumsden, L. S. (1994). *Student motivation to learn.* (ERIC Digest No. 92). Eugene, OR: ERIC Clearinghouse on Educational Management.

Marzano, R. J. (2007). *The art and science of teaching: A comprehensive framework for effective instruction.* Alexandria, VA: ASCD.

Marzano, R. J. (2009). Setting the record straight on "high-yield" strategies. *Phi Delta Kappan, 91*(1), 30–37.

Marzano, R. J., Frontier, T., & Livingston, D. (2011). *Effective supervision: Supporting the art and science of teaching.* Alexandria, VA: ASCD.

Marzano, R. J., Kendall, J. S., & Gaddy, B. B. (1999). *Essential knowledge: The debate over what American students should know.* Aurora, CO: Mid-continent Regional Education Laboratory.

Marzano, R. J., Marzano, J. S., & Pickering, D. J. (2003). *Classroom management that works: Research-based strategies for every teacher.* Alexandria, VA: ASCD.

Marzano, R. J., Pickering, D. J., & Pollock, J. E. (2001). *Classroom instruction that works: Research-based strategies for increasing student achievement.* Alexandria, VA: ASCD.

Marzano, R. J., Waters, T., & McNulty, B. A. (2005). *School leadership that works: From research to results.* Alexandria, VA: ASCD.

McKinsey & Company. (2007). *How the world's best-performing school systems come out on top.* New York: Author.

McKinsey & Company. (2009). *The economic impact of the achievement gap in America's schools.* Washington, DC: Author.

McTighe, J., & Wiggins, G. (2013). *Essential questions: Opening doors to student understanding.* Alexandria, VA: ASCD.

Meisels, S. J., & Liaw, F. (1993). Failure in grade: Do retained students catch up? *Journal of Educational Research, 87*(2), 69–77.

Mielke, P., & Frontier, T. (2012, November). Keeping improvement in mind. *Educational Leadership, 70*(3), 10–13.

Milesi, C., & Gamoran, A. (2006). Effects of class size and instruction on kindergarten achievement. *Educational Evaluation and Policy Analysis, 28*(4), 287–313.

Miller, G. A. (1956). The magical number seven, plus or minus two: Some limits on our capacity to process information. *Psychological Review, 63*(2), 81–97.

Mouza, C. (2008). Learning with laptops: Implementation and outcomes in an urban, under-privileged school. *Journal of Research on Technology in Education, 40*(4), 447–472.

Mynard, J., & Sorflaten, R. (2002). *Independent learning in your classroom.* Paper presented at the TESOL Arabia 2002 conference.

National Center for Public Policy and Higher Education. (2010). *The gap between enrolling in college and being ready for college.* Author.

National Commission on Excellence in Education. (1983). *A nation at risk: The imperative for educational reform.* Washington, DC: Author.

National Governors Association Center for Best Practices & Council of Chief State School Officers. (2010). *Common Core State Standards*. Washington, DC: Authors.

Nisbett, R. E. (2009). *Intelligence and how to get it: Why schools and cultures count*. New York: Norton.

North Central Regional Educational Laboratory. (1995). Critical issue: Working toward student self-direction and personal efficacy as educational goals. Retrieved from http://www.ncrel.org/sdrs/areas/issues/students/learning/lr200.htm

O'Connor, K. (2002). *How to grade for learning: Linking grades to standards* (2nd ed.). Thousand Oaks, CA: Corwin Press.

Organisation for Economic Co-operation and Development (OECD). (2010). *Programme for International Student Assessment (PISA) 2010 results*. Paris: Author.

Osberg, K. M. (1997). *Constructivism in practice: The case for meaning-making in the virtual world* (Unpublished doctoral dissertation). University of Washington, Seattle. Retrieved from http://www.hitl.washington.edu/publications/r-97-47/title.html

O'Shea, M. R. (2005). *From standards to success: A guide for school leaders*. Alexandria, VA: ASCD.

Patall, E. A., Cooper, H., & Allen, A. B. (2010). Extending the school day or school year: A systematic review of research (1985–2009). *Review of Educational Research, 80*(3), 401–436. doi: 10.3102/0034654310377086

Payne, C. M. (2008). *So much reform, so little change: The persistence of failure in urban schools*. Cambridge, MA: Harvard Education Press.

Pedersen, S., & Williams, D. (2004). A comparison of assessment practices and their effects on learning and motivation in a student-centered learning environment. *Journal of Educational Multimedia and Hypermedia, 13*(3), 283–306.

Pennington, H. (2006, October 26). *Expanding learning time in high schools*. Washington, DC: Center for American Progress. Available: http://www.americanprogress.org/wp-content/uploads/issues/2006/10/pdf/extended_learning_report.pdf

Penuel, W. R. (2006). Implementation and effects of 1:1 computing initiatives: A research synthesis. *Journal of Research on Technology in Education, 38*(3), 229–348.

Perez, A. D., & Hirschman, C. (2009). Estimating net interracial mobility in the United States: A residual methods approach. *Sociological Methodology, 39*, 31–71.

Pew. (2011, April 20). Driving to 54.5 MPG: The history of fuel economy. Available: http://www.pewenvironment.org/news-room/fact-sheets/driving-to-545-mpg-the-history-of-fuel-economy-329037

Pink, D. H. (2009). *Drive: The surprising truth about what motivates us*. New York: Riverhead Books.

Pope, D. C. (2001). *Doing school: How we are creating a generation of stressed out, materialistic, and miseducated students*. New Haven, CT: Yale University Press.

Popham, J. W. (2008). *Transformative assessment*. Alexandria, VA: ASCD.

Ravitch, D. (2010). *The death and life of the great American school system: How testing and choice are undermining education*. New York: Basic Books.

Rickabaugh, J. (2012). *The learning independence continuum*. Pewaukee, WI: The Institute @ CESA #1.

Robinson, K. (2010). Changing paradigms. Retrieved from http://www.thersa.org/events/rsaanimate/animate/rsa-animate-changing-paradigms

Rogers, K. B. (2002). *Re-forming gifted education: Matching the program to the child*. Scottsdale, AZ: Great Potential Press.

Romanowski, M. H. (2004, Summer). Student obsession with grades and achievement. *Kappa Delta Pi Record, 40*(4), 149–151.

Rosenthal, R., & Jacobson, L. (1968). *Pygmalion in the classroom: Teacher expectation and pupils' intellectual development*. Austin, TX: Holt, Rinehart & Winston.

Russell, V. J., Ainley M., & Frydenberg, E. (2005, October 28). *Schooling issues digest: Student motivation and engagement*. Australian Government, Department of Education, Employment and Workplace Relations. Retrieved from http://www.dest.gov.au/NR/rdonlyres/89068B42-7520-45AB-A965-F01328C95268/8138/SchoolingIssuesDigestMotivationandEngagement.pdf

Ryan, A. M., Gheen, M. H., & Midgley, C. (1998). Why do some students avoid asking for help? An examination of the interplay among students, academic efficacy, teachers' social–emotional role, and the classroom goal structure. *Journal of Educational Psychology, 90,* 528–535.

Sax, L. (2007). *Boys adrift: The five factors driving the growing epidemic of unmotivated boys and underachieving young men*. New York: Basic Books.

Sax, L. (2010). *Girls on the edge: The four factors driving the new crisis for girls*. New York: Basic Books.

Schlechty, P. C. (2001). *Shaking up the schoolhouse: How to support and sustain educational innovation*. San Francisco: Jossey-Bass.

Schlechty, P. C. (2002). *Working on the work: An action plan for teachers, principals, and superintendents*. San Francisco: Jossey-Bass.

Schlechty, P. C. (2011). *Engaging students: The next level of working on the work*. San Francisco: Jossey-Bass.

Schunk, D. (1991). Self-efficacy and academic motivation. *Educational Psychologist, 26*(3–4), 207–231. doi: 10.1080/00461520.1991.9653133

Self-Brown, S. R., & Mathews, S. (2003). Effects of classroom structure on student achievement goal orientation. *Journal of Educational Research, 97*(2), 106–112.

Shepard, L. A. (2000). The role of assessment in a learning culture. *Educational Researcher, 29*(7), 4–14.

Silver, H., Dewing, R.T., & Perini, M.J. (2012). *The core six: Essential strategies for achieving excellence with the Common Core.* Alexandria, VA: ASCD.

Simmons, E. (2004). The Writing Project and Tulsa schools collaborate for school reform that works. *The Voice, 9*(3). Available: http://www.nwp.org/cs/public/print/resource/1961

Simon, H. A., & Chase, W. G. (1973). Skill in chess. *American Scientist, 61,* 394–403.

Slavin, R. E. (1987). Ability grouping and student achievement in elementary schools: A best-evidence synthesis. *Review of Educational Research, 57*(3), 293–336.

Steele, C. M., Spencer, S. J., & Aronson, J. (2002). Contending with group image: The psychology of stereotype and social identity threat. *Advances in Experimental Social Psychology, 34,* 379–440.

Stefanou, C. R., Perencevich, K. C., DiCintio, M., & Turner, J. C. (2004). Supporting autonomy in the classroom: Ways teachers encourage student decision making and ownership. *Educational Psychologist, 39*(2), 97–110.

Stengel, R. (2009, April 15). Arne Duncan: The apostle of reform. *Time.* Available: http://www.time.com/time/magazine/article/0,9171,1891734,00.html

Stiggins, R. J. (2001). *Student-involved classroom assessment* (3rd ed.). Upper Saddle River, NJ: Merrill/Prentice Hall.

Stiggins, R. J. (2002). Assessment crisis! The absence of assessment *FOR* learning. *Phi Delta Kappan, 83*(10), 758–765.

Stiggins, R. J., (2004). New assessment beliefs for a new school mission. *Phi Delta Kappan, 86*(1), 22–27.

Stiggins, R. J. (2006). Assessment through the student's eyes. *Educational Leadership, 65*(9), 22–26.

Stiggins, R. J., & Chappuis, J. (2005). Using student-involved classroom assessment to close achievement gaps. *Theory into Practice, 44*(1), 11–18.

Strong, M. (2011). *The highly qualified teacher: What is teacher quality and how do you measure it?* New York: Teachers College Press.

Strong, R., Silver, H. F., & Robinson, A. (1995, September). What do students want (and what really motivates them)? *Educational Leadership, 53*(12), 8–12. Retrieved from http://www.bcatml.org/POT/strong_silver_motivation.pdf

Stronge, J. H. (2010). *Effective teachers = student achievement: What the research says.* Larchmont, NY: Eye on Education.

Tamim, R. M., Bernard, R. M., Barokhovski, E., Abrami, P. C., & Schmid, R. F. (2011, March). What forty years of research says about the impact of technology on learning: A second-order meta-analysis and validation study. *Review of Educational Research, 81*(1), 4–28. doi: 10.3102/0034654310393361

Tucker, M. S. (Ed.). (2011). *Surpassing Shanghai: An agenda for American education built on the world's leading systems.* Cambridge, MA: Harvard Education Press.

U.S. Department of Education. (2005). *Single-sex versus coeducational schooling: A systematic review.* Washington, DC: Author.

Voke, H. (2002, February). Motivating students to learn. *ASCD Infobrief, 2*(28). Retrieved from http://www.ascd.org/readingroom/infobrief/200202_issue28.html

Voltz, D. L., Sims, M. J., & Nelson, B. (2010). *Connecting teachers, students, and standards: Strategies for success in diverse and inclusive classrooms.* Alexandria, VA: ASCD.

Wigfield, A., & Wagner, A. L. (2005). Competence, motivation, and identity development during adolescence. In A. Elliot & C. S. Dweck (Eds.), *Handbook of competence and motivation* (pp. 222–239). New York: Guilford Press.

Wiggins, G., & McTighe, J. (2005). *Understanding by design* (Expanded 2nd ed.). Alexandria, VA: ASCD.

Witte, J. F., Carlson, D., Cowen, J. M., Fleming, D. J., & Wolf, P. J. (2011). *MPCP longitudinal educational growth study: Fourth year report.* Report of the School Choice Demonstration Project. Fayetteville, AR: University of Arkansas.

Wolfe, P. (1987, February). What the "Seven Steps Lesson Plan" isn't! *Educational Leadership, 44*(5), 70–71.

Worthy, J. (2010). Only the names have been changed: Ability grouping revisited. *Urban Review, 42*(4), 271–295.

Yeager, D. S., & Walton, G. M. (2011). Social-psychological interventions in education: They're not magic. *Review of Educational Research, 81*(2), 267–301.

Zimmerman, B. J., Bandura, A., & Martinez-Pons, M. (1992). Self-motivation for academic attainment: The role of self-efficacy beliefs and personal goal setting. *American Educational Research Journal, 29*(3), 663–676. doi: 10.2307/1163261

Index

Note: Page references followed by an italicized *f* indicate material in figures.

About the Authors

Tony Frontier, Ph.D., is an Assistant Professor of Doctoral Leadership Studies and Director of Teacher Education at Cardinal Stritch University. He is coauthor of the ASCD book *Effective Supervision: Supporting the Art and Science of Teaching* and has been recognized by Marquette University as the College of Education's Outstanding Young Alumnus, by Wisconsin ASCD as the state's Outstanding Young Educator, and by ASCD as an Emerging Leader. He can be reached at acfrontier@stritch.edu

Jim Rickabaugh, Ph.D. is the Director of The Institute @ CESA 1, whose work is focused on innovation in schools. He was named the AASA Minnesota State Superintendent of the Year in 1995 and Wisconsin State Superintendent of the Year in 2008. Jim has been an adjunct faculty member at the University of Wisconsin–Madison, where he taught courses in the areas of educational administration and educational leadership. He can be reached at jim.rickabaugh@gmail.com